You Are Wonderfully Made

You Are Wonderfully Made

Dr ant

CONTENTS

Table of Contents

You Are Wonderfully Made
A Faith-Based Approach
by
Dr. ant

You Are Wonderfully Made: A Faith-Based Approach

Contents

Introduction

The Catholic Church stands at a pivotal moment in history, one where cultural shifts challenge traditional values and beliefs at every turn. For young adults and teenagers, navigating this landscape can feel overwhelming, where each day presents a fresh array of questions about identity, purpose, and the meaning of life. It is within this stirring context that the Theology of the Body curriculum finds its essential purpose—a beacon to guide, illuminate, and offer paths of understanding rooted in faith, respect, and love.

The importance of the Theology of the Body cannot be overstated, especially in a world where the notion of self has become increasingly fluid and often distorted. Stemming from the teachings of Pope Saint John Paul II, it offers a profound and comprehensive understanding of the human person, focusing deeply on our identity not just as individuals but as beings created in the likeness of God. This curriculum strives to reconnect us with this core identity, building on the notion that our bodies are not mere vessels but integral to our spiritual and relational existence.

Considering the target audience for this book—Roman Catholics, Knights of Columbus, young adults, and teenagers—the need for such a curriculum becomes even more pronounced. For those standing at the crossroad between youth and adulthood, or those committed to guiding them, understanding the relationship between body and soul, between divine intention and human action, provides an unmatched framework for personal development. It's about anchoring faith into every aspect of life, transforming everyday experiences into moments of divine grace.

The Knights of Columbus, with their longstanding history of service and commitment to faith, are uniquely positioned to spearhead this curriculum. Their mission aligns seamlessly with the teachings of the Theology of the Body—it's a call to uphold dignity, champion love, and foster respect in all interactions. This book aims to equip them with the insights and tools necessary to engage young minds and hearts effectively, empowering them with not only knowledge but also the conviction to apply these teachings in life.

The curriculum of Theology of the Body is an odyssey—one that invites young people to explore the depths of their own existence, challenge societal norms that conflict with their faith, and emerge with a robust sense of purpose and commitment. In such an exploration, it's vital to teach them about love not merely as an emotion but a vocation, calling for responsibility and authenticity. These principles serve as bedrock for building healthy relationships, whether familial, platonic, or romantic, characterized by mutual respect and understanding.

At its core, Theology of the Body emphasizes that our physical existence has sacramental value. The body is not just a shell but manifests holiness, a truth reflected in every sacramental act, from the Eucharist to Matrimony. Emphasizing this aspect helps young adults see their own physicality as a part of God's plan, inviting them to live with a sense of reverence not often found in secular discourse.

Yet, in espousing these values, the curriculum must also be adaptable, addressing the real issues young people face today. Whether discerning a vocation, understanding the role of chastity, or navigating pressures from peers and media, these teachings should offer practical guidance imbued with compassion and truth. Young people need to see faith as a living element of daily existence, not an abstract concept relegated to catechism classes or Sunday Mass.

In embracing this curriculum, readers will also explore how modern challenges intersect with ancient truths. The world of technology, for instance, presents unique dilemmas yet also opens doors for new expressions of faith. Understanding and navigating this digital landscape responsibly is crucial—young Catholics are called to be in the world, not of it, striking a balance between participation and preservation of faith.

This introduction isn't just an invitation to explore these topics but a charge to take action. By choosing to engage with the Theology of the Body, you're not merely learning; you're participating in a transformative journey, one that has the power to reshape not just individual lives but the larger community of faith. A life lived in harmony with these teachings becomes a testament of faith in action, illuminating the path for others and fostering a culture of life.

Thus, the curriculum aims to enrich not only personal understanding but the broader mission of the Church and the Knights of Columbus, creating leaders who are not only knowledgeable but also empathetic and courageous. These leaders will not only guide others but inspire them to embrace and cherish the divine gift that is the human body, nurturing a community grounded in love and respect for all.

Chapter 1: Understanding Theology of the Body

Theology of the Body unveils a profound vision of the human person, deeply rooted in divine wisdom and love. It's more than just a framework; it's a journey that invites us to see our bodies as sacred, woven into the fabric of God's divine plan. Reflecting on our creation in God's image, this theology challenges us to rethink how we perceive ourselves and others, emphasizing that each body narrates the story of His love and purpose. Embracing this understanding, especially for young adults guided by the Knights of Columbus, isn't merely adopting a set of beliefs but becoming part of a transformative movement that respects, dignifies, and recognizes the holiness in every aspect of human existence. It's an invitation to engage, educate, and empower youth to live out these truths in their daily lives, leading them to a more authentic and fulfilling relationship with God and one another. This chapter lays the foundation for embracing a life where faith and the human experience dance in harmony, revealing the beauty and sacredness inherent in our physical existence.

Overview of Theology of the Body

Theology of the Body, a profound teaching developed by Pope John Paul II, delves into the very essence of what it means to be human in light of divine purpose. At its core, this theology invites us to explore the relationship between body and spirit, demonstrating how the physical self is not merely a vessel but an integral component of our spiritual journey. It's a holistic view that encourages a deep understanding of our identity, our relationships, and our ultimate calling to love.

The core premise of the Theology of the Body is that the human body has a specific meaning, one that is deeply connected to the spiritual and the divine. This isn't just about our physicality but about how our bodies reflect our innermost being and divine likeness. In a world that's often quick to separate the spiritual from the physical, this teaching calls us back to a unified vision of humanity where every part of us plays a role in our holiness and redemption.

Initially presented during a series of papal audiences, Theology of the Body encompasses diverse themes, yet at its heart, it's a contemplation of what it means for us to be created male and female. It's not merely about sexuality or physical relationships, although these are significant aspects of the discussion. Rather, it's about understanding God's original design and how through our bodies, we enter into relationships that mirror the divine love and communion.

Within the framework of this teaching, marriage emerges as a profound reflection of God's covenantal love. But the insights go beyond the married state. The Theology of the Body offers a vision that's universal, addressing how single, religious, and married life each reveal unique aspects of God's plan. It's a call to recognize our bodies' sacramental nature, a visible sign of invisible grace, urging us to engage with our human experiences more fully and faithfully.

The Christian understanding of personhood places immense value on human dignity. Here, every individual is crafted with love and purpose, reflecting the image of God. Through this theology, we are invited to see beyond the superficial and materialistic views that often dominate contemporary culture. It's a push against reducing human beings to mere objects or priorities that can be commodified or dismissed.

Reflecting on love as the central calling of the human person, Theology of the Body speaks beyond doctrinal instructions and into the vibrant reality of lived experiences. Young adults and teenagers, the primary audience for this curriculum, face a world filled with confusing messages about identity and love. This teaching offers clarity, presenting love not as a fleeting emotion but as an enduring commitment grounded in self-gift and communion.

For the Knights of Columbus, the guardians and promoters of this curriculum, it's crucial to convey that this is not a new set of rules to follow, but a liberation into the fullness of our Christian dignity. By weaving these insights into the formation of youth, the Knights can foster a generation ready to embrace the challenges and joys of authentic love and community. This education is not simply academic but aims to transform the way we live and interact with others.

Theology of the Body also addresses the concepts of shame, vulnerability, and sincerity of heart in their rightful places. It acknowledges the realities of human weakness while never straying from the truth of redemption and grace. Through examining these aspects, young people learn to approach their personal faults and societal struggles with compassion and hope.

Inherent in the Theology of the Body is an invitation to reflect on our personal journeys and the collective pilgrimage of the Church toward sainthood. It calls for an interior transformation, urging every believer to see the world not only with their eyes but through the eyes of faith. This vision proposes a counterculture of life and love, challenging prevalent narratives that often dehumanize or depersonalize human interaction.

To incorporate these teachings effectively into teenage and young adult programs, careful attention must be paid to how these theological reflections can bridge understanding between the ancient truths and present-day challenges. Rather than treat the body and spirit as separate spheres, Theology of the Body sets the foundation for an integrated approach, paving the way for authentic, joyful living in every state of life.

In conclusion, the "Overview of Theology of the Body" is more than an intellectual exploration. It's an invitation to experience humanity and divinity intertwined, urging the Knights of Columbus to inspire the young toward a future where dignity and love are the hallmarks of Christian living. This understanding forms a springboard for the comprehensive formation envisioned in the chapters to follow, always striving to deepen the faith and enliven the spirit of generations to come.

Foundations in the Holy Bible

Understanding the foundations of Theology of the Body requires us to delve into the sacred scriptures of the Holy Bible, which serve as the cornerstone for its teachings. The Bible is not just a collection of ancient texts; it is a living document providing insights into our relationship with God and with each other. It is within these texts that the intrinsic link between our physical bodies and spiritual beings is woven, forming the basis for the Theology of the Body. This teaching is intensely rooted in the belief that our bodies are not mere vessels, but a profound expression of the divine.

In the beginning, the Book of Genesis introduces us to the Creation narrative. Here, it tells how God created man in His own image, male and female He created them. This foundational passage highlights the dignity of the human person, establishing that we are a reflection of God's own nature. This scriptural affirmation emphasizes the goodness of the body, dismissing any notion that the material world is inherently inferior to the spiritual. Rather, it asserts that our bodies have a divine purpose and are essential to our identity as humans.

Furthermore, the covenant relationship between God and humanity is vividly demonstrated through the story of Adam and Eve. In their union, we see a paradigmatic model of relationality that is not merely symbolic but inherently physical. When Adam declares, "This at last is bone of my bones and flesh of my flesh," he acknowledges the unity and communion intended by Creator. This implies that our relationship with one another and with God is not abstract but incarnational, emphasizing the sacredness of bodily encounters.

Moving through the biblical narrative, we encounter the Law and the Prophets, where God's care for humanity continues to unfold. The laws presented to Moses on Mount Sinai, though often perceived as restrictive, are actually manifestations of God's commitment to guiding His people. These commandments serve to protect the dignity and integrity of the human body and soul, calling us to holiness. They remind us that our physical actions are imbued with spiritual significance, shaping our path to become more aligned with divine will.

The Psalms, with their poetic beauty, also reflect on the sanctity of the human body. For instance, Psalm 139 eloquently speaks of being "fearfully and wonderfully made," celebrating the intricate design of the human person. The psalmist recognizes that the wonder of creation is not confined to the natural world but resides in each person's very being. This profound recognition invites us to a deeper appreciation and respect for our own bodies and those of others.

One cannot overlook the prophetic voices in the Old Testament who called the people of Israel back to right relationship with God and each other. The prophet Isaiah, for example, spoke of a suffering servant who would bear the infirmities of the people. This imagery offers a glimpse into the redemption and healing that comes through the body, prefiguring the ultimate act of love in the New Testament. The prophets collectively reinforce the call to see beyond mere flesh, to the spiritual realities our bodies point towards.

The culmination of these Old Testament teachings is fulfilled in the New Testament, where the Word becomes flesh in the person of Jesus Christ. This incarnation is the ultimate divine endorsement of the human body, revealing the interconnection between divinity and humanity. In Christ, we see the perfect harmony of body and spirit, as He lived His earthly life. His physical suffering, death, and resurrection illustrate the redemptive potential of the human body, offering a profound theological insight: our bodies are integral to our salvation history.

Moreover, Jesus' interactions with people during His ministry further emphasize the importance of the body. His healings and miracles often involved touching and being touched, underscoring the sanctity of physical presence. In these encounters, Jesus restored not just physical health but wholeness, reminding us that our bodies are temples of the Holy Spirit. In this way, Jesus models for us how to live authentically in our own bodies, serving as instruments of love, compassion, and reconciliation.

The apostolic letters, especially those of St. Paul, provide additional theological deepening. For instance, in First Corinthians, Paul refers to our bodies as "members of Christ" and "temples of the Holy Spirit," reiterating the call to treat our bodies with reverence and integrity. These letters address communal and personal holiness, integrating the physical and spiritual dimensions of life. Paul's writing moves beyond cultural norms of his time, holding the body in high esteem and challenging us to do likewise.

Biblical teachings, then, frame Theology of the Body as a call to embrace our humanity in its fullness, respecting the profound mystery of our bodily existence as a gift from God. It compels us to see ourselves and others not merely as physical entities but as embodiments of divine love. Grounded in scripture, this theology provides a lens through which we can understand our place in the world and our destiny in the divine plan.

In synthesizing these scriptural foundations, the Holy Bible provides a rich narrative that underscores the dignity, purpose, and beauty of the human body. It invites young Catholics, and Knights of Columbus in particular, to appreciate their physicality as a vital aspect of their spiritual journey. Through this understanding, we can teach the younger generation to treat their own and each other's bodies with the reverence they deserve, fostering lives that reflect the glory for which God created them. This profound scriptural grounding enriches the mission of developing a Theology of the Body curriculum, encouraging teenagers and young adults to discover the sacredness inherent in human embodiment.

Chapter 2: The Knights of Columbus and Their Role

Building upon the foundations of the Theology of the Body, the Knights of Columbus stand as vanguards in nurturing the spiritual and moral growth of young Catholics. Embodying a mission reminiscent of chivalrous guardians, these knights are dedicated to molding hearts and minds through truth and love. Their role is not just ceremonial but profoundly impactful, offering guidance as educators who decode complex teachings and present them in ways that resonate with the young, making them profound allies in faith formation. In harnessing their commitment and resources, the Knights provide an educational framework that helps teenagers and young adults navigate the virtues and challenges laid out by our faith, ensuring a future generation well-versed in theological and ethical understanding. This pivotal role of the Knights not only strengthens individual faith journeys but enriches the entire Catholic community by fostering a deeper, collective commitment to live with integrity and conviction.

Mission of the Knights of Columbus

The Knights of Columbus, an organization founded on the principles of charity, unity, fraternity, and patriotism, has long played a vital role within the Catholic Church. Their mission, deeply rooted in the teachings of the Church and inspired by unwavering commitment, extends to forming a strong moral and spiritual foundation for the community they serve. Central to their work is the mission of promoting the Theology of the Body, a profound teaching that elucidates the beauty and dignity of the human person as created in the image of God.

In today's rapidly changing world, young people find themselves confronted with myriad challenges and questions about their identity, worth, and purpose. The Knights have taken it upon themselves to become beacons of light, helping to guide teenagers and young adults through these complexities by providing them with resources rooted in the Theology of the Body. This mission isn't just about imparting knowledge; it's about fostering an environment where young people can discover their unique value as individuals made in the likeness of their Creator.

However, the task is not without its challenges. The landscape of modern society is replete with messages that often conflict with the values upheld by the Knights. Yet, it is precisely these challenges that underscore the importance of the Knights' mission. With steadfast resolve, they are dedicated to offering a counter-narrative — one that affirms life, dignity, and the sacredness of the human body.

At the heart of the Knights' mission is a dedication to fostering a true understanding of love and relationships through the lens of the Theology of the Body. This involves not only teaching about the responsibilities that come with love but also helping young minds to see love as a vocation — a divine calling that can manifest in many forms, including marriage, celibacy, and community service. Their instructional approach carries an empathetic tone, resonating with the gentle strength found in the teachings of the saints.

The Knights are particularly focused on making these teachings accessible and understandable. Understanding that young adults and teenagers relate to authenticity, they strive to live out the values they teach, providing a living example of what it means to be a Knight of Columbus. By providing mentorship and fostering open dialogue, they create an educational experience that encourages questioning and exploration while maintaining a firm grounding in faith's truth.

One of the primary methods the Knights use to achieve their mission is through engaging programs and initiatives that align with the Theology of the Body. They host retreats, workshops, and classes that provide young people with the tools they need to not only grasp the abstract concepts of this theology but also apply it in their daily lives. These programs aim to empower individuals to see their bodies not as mere vessels but as temples of the Holy Spirit, reflecting the divine plan in everyday actions and choices.

Moreover, the Knights of Columbus understand the power of community in supporting this mission. They emphasize the importance of building strong, faith-based networks where individuals can find support, understanding, and encouragement. Through organizing local councils and community events, they create spaces where faith can be deepened and lived out in fellowship with others.

The mission also extends beyond teaching and community building. Advocacy forms a crucial component of their work. In advocating for pro-life teachings and actions, the Knights reinforce the message of inherent human dignity from conception to natural death. This advocacy work not only serves as a public testament to their values but also inspires young people to become advocates for life and dignity in their own rights.

To continuously evolve and respond to the ever-changing social climate, the Knights also engage in ongoing self-reflection and education. They actively seek feedback from the youth they mentor and the communities they serve. By doing so, they ensure their mission remains relevant and impactful, aligning with the core teachings of the Catholic faith while addressing contemporary issues faced by young Catholics today.

Ultimately, the mission of the Knights of Columbus is about more than teaching doctrines; it's about empowering individuals to embrace their identity as children of God, equipped with the knowledge and strength to navigate life's challenges with grace and faith. In doing so, they strive to not only build up the Church but also transform society by nurturing a generation grounded in truth and love.

As they carry out this sacred mission, the Knights remain inspired by the words of Christ and the example of the saints who have walked before them. Their unwavering faith and dedication serve as a reminder that the mission of the Knights of Columbus is indeed a calling — one that has significant importance both within the Church and society at large. It is a mission that resonates with hope, a mission that holds the promise of renewal, a mission that eagerly invites all who are willing to participate in building a culture of life and love for the glory of God.

Educator's Guide for Knights

The task of educating young hearts and minds in the truth and beauty of Theology of the Body is both a great privilege and a profound responsibility. As Knights of Columbus, this mission becomes a beckoning call to shape not only knowledgeable individuals but also persons of virtue and character. The "Educator's Guide for Knights" serves as a compass, charting a course that can transform society by shaping the lives of younger generations.

At the core of this guide lies an understanding that teaching is more than just imparting information—it's about guiding the young toward a deeper relationship with God through understanding their own sacred dignity. The Knights are called to plant seeds of wisdom and virtue, nurturing them to flourish. This involves creating environments where discussions about faith, identity, love, and responsibility not only happen but are encouraged in meaningful ways.

Theological grounding is crucial. As educators, you must draw insights from the Scriptures and the Church's teachings, grounding every session in the truths elaborated by saints and theologians alike. It's about connecting the profound reflections of Theology of the Body with the real-life struggles and questions that the youth face. Sharing personal reflections and testimonies about how understanding the Theology of the Body has been transformative in one's life can bridge these connections.

The key is to let faith speak to the hearts. Encourage questions, listen actively, and respect the different spiritual journeys of each young adult and teenager. Use stories from the lives of the saints, parables from the Bible, and even personal anecdotes to drive home points in a way that is relatable and impactful. This empathetic approach will allow young learners to see the relevance of Theology of the Body in their own lives.

Engagement and interaction are paramount. Encourage participatory lessons where students are not passive recipients but active contributors. Consider integrating group discussions, role-playing, or interactive faith-based projects that prompt the youth to explore the themes of love, sacrifice, and vocation actively. This could be enhanced through various artistic outlets such as music, drama, or visual arts, which resonate deeply with young audiences and bring the concepts of Theology of the Body to life.

The journey of forming young minds through Theology of the Body requires adaptability. Recognize that each group you instruct might understand or respond to teachings differently. Thus, flexibility and creativity in teaching methods are vital. Tailor your approach to age groups, backgrounds, and individual personalities for optimal impact. Consider technological tools and digital resources that can support and modernize your teachings without compromising the spiritual essence.

Remember, this is a collaborative effort. Engage with parents, guardians, and other members of the community to create a support system that perpetuates the learning and living of Theology of the Body principles beyond the sessions. When young people see a community living out these tenets genuinely, it gives the teachings a true sense of realism and attainability.

Nurturing the spirit of discernment is another vital component. It's essential to guide young individuals in recognizing their unique vocations and how they fit into God's larger story. Help them to see this discernment as an ongoing dialogue with God, one that is patient and filled with moments of silence, reflection, and prayer. This way, they learn to align their choices with a life of service and love.

In every teaching moment, strive to inspire young hearts to dream of a world transformed by love. Instill a vision that sees the human body as a sacramental gift from God, made to express love and commit to others selflessly. As Knights, your role is to model this love actively so the youth may see, believe, and live it out daily.

The "Educator's Guide for Knights" is more than just a manual; it's a call to action. Embrace it wholeheartedly, knowing that through your efforts, you're shaping leaders in faith—sons and daughters who will carry forward this mission of love and integrity, echoing its principles in their families, workplaces, and communities.

Many challenges await, but remember, the harvest is plenty. You are not alone in this mission. The fraternity of the Knights stands beside you, strengthened by prayer and shared purpose. Together, let us step forward, guided by faith, united in love, educating souls for a brighter tomorrow.

Chapter 3: The Human Person as Image of God

In contemplating the human person as the image of God, we delve deep into a central tenet of our faith that illuminates the profound dignity inherent in every individual. God created us uniquely, infusing our very being with his essence and love. This divine likeness, captured in the sacred texts, affirms our calling to reflect his goodness in our actions and relationships. We aren't just physical beings; we're spiritual entities with an innate capacity for love, grace, and communion with the divine. Through the lens of science and faith, we recognize the extraordinary nature of humanity as a remarkable intersection of body and spirit. Our unique attributes—our intellect, creativity, and capacity for self-gift—magnify the Creator's hand in our lives. Young Catholics, embracing this understanding is crucial in a world eager to define worth through temporal measures. As we recognize each person's divine imprint, we foster a community grounded in love, mutual respect, and the mission to live out this truth in a way that transforms both our hearts and the world around us.

Biblical Insights on Human Dignity

When reflecting on the concept of human dignity, the Bible offers profound insights that reveal the intrinsic value of every individual. At the heart of this exploration is the belief that each person is created in the "image and likeness of God" as described in Genesis. This foundational biblical declaration establishes human dignity as inherent, not conferred by societal status, accomplishments, or material wealth. Each person's worth is non-negotiable, as it is rooted in divine creation. This notion invites us to see ourselves and others from a perspective that transcends worldly judgments, urging us to honor the sanctity of life in all its forms.

The narrative of creation in the Book of Genesis marks the beginning of the profound truth of human dignity. Here, God breathes life into Adam and Eve, setting humans apart from the rest of creation. This divine act signifies more than the beginning of human life; it establishes an eternal relationship between the Creator and humanity. It highlights that human dignity is tied to our capacity for a relationship with God, one that is built on love, trust, and communion. This relationship is not a privilege for some but a calling for all, reflecting the universality of human dignity.

Throughout scripture, various passages reaffirm this intrinsic worth. Take the Psalms, for instance. In Psalm 139, we are reminded of our unique creation: "For you formed my inward parts; you knitted me together in my mother's womb." This intimate image of God's creativity stimulates a deeper understanding of individual significance and reinforces the idea that every person, from conception to natural death, is precious in the eyes of God. Such passages challenge us to appreciate the beauty and complexity of every human life.

Moreover, the prophets of the Old Testament continually emphasize justice and care for the marginalized as expressions of respect for human dignity. Take, for example, the plea from Isaiah to "defend the oppressed, take up the cause of the fatherless, plead the case of the widow." These calls to action reflect God's enduring commitment to human dignity and provide a model for our own responses to social injustices. By following these teachings, we actively participate in God's vision of a just and equitable world.

Jesus Christ's own life and ministry further illuminate the concept of human dignity. By choosing to dwell among us, taking on human form, and experiencing our struggles and joys, Jesus imbues human life with sanctity and significance. The Gospels are replete with examples of Jesus' encounters with society's outcasts—the sick, the poor, the sinners. He didn't merely acknowledge their existence; he extended love, healing, and forgiveness to them, affirming their worth in the eyes of God and inviting them into community. Through these interactions, Jesus reveals that true dignity transcends societal labels and prejudices.

A particularly notable instance is Jesus' parable about the Good Samaritan. Here, we see a powerful call to recognize and protect the dignity of others, even those we might consider different or distant. This story transcends cultural and religious boundaries, challenging listeners to show mercy and care without hesitation. In this way, the parable becomes a timeless model of compassion, urging us to see God's image in every neighbor regardless of differences.

Another dimension of understanding human dignity biblically comes from recognizing our call to stewardship. In being appointed stewards of creation, humans are entrusted with the responsibility to care for and protect the world. This role reaffirms our dignity as co-workers in Creation with God. It emphasizes a communal aspect of dignity, where our actions profoundly impact others and the environment. Through responsible stewardship, we affirm the interconnectedness of all creation and our shared destiny.

Furthermore, Paul's letters to the early Christian communities offer insights into maintaining dignity amidst persecution and adversity. In the letter to the Corinthians, Paul speaks eloquently about the body being a temple of the Holy Spirit. This metaphor not only highlights the sacredness of the physical self but also calls believers to live out their dignity through purity, respect, and love. Paul's teachings remind us that human dignity encompasses both the spiritual and physical realms, promoting a holistic view of human existence.

The book of Revelation, often viewed through the lens of eschatology, also presents a vision of dignity restored fully in the new heaven and earth. The imagery used—of God dwelling among His people where "he will wipe every tear from their eyes"—paints a picture of ultimate dignity, where human suffering and injustices are redeemed. This vision offers hope, assuring believers that dignity is not merely an earthly reality but one that finds its complete expression in eternity.

These biblical teachings find relevance today as they challenge us to confront and address contemporary issues such as discrimination, exploitation, and war that threaten to undermine human dignity. By anchoring our understanding of dignity in the divine image, we can navigate these challenges with renewed resolve and moral clarity. The wisdom of scripture becomes a guiding light, urging us to act with faith and courage in a world needing compassion and justice.

For the Knights of Columbus and the wider Roman Catholic community, these insights are not just theological ideals but practical guides for everyday action. The call to protect and cherish human dignity is deeply embedded in the order's commitments to charity, unity, and fraternity. By embodying these teachings, the Knights provide a living example of the Church's mission to uphold the sacredness of human life and to act as bearers of hope and peace in the world.

In light of these Biblical insights, young adults and teenagers are invited to explore and embrace their own dignity and that of others. In understanding their worth as children of God, they are better equipped to face life's challenges with confidence and integrity. The Church, through its teachings and community support, offers guidance and companionship in this journey, fostering an environment where dignity can thrive.

Ultimately, the biblical perspective on human dignity presents a transformative truth that has the power to change lives. It's an invitation to see the world and each other through God's compassionate eyes, recognizing the shared divine image in everyone. This acknowledgment serves as the cornerstone for building just communities where peace, love, and respect flourish—a vision rooted in the heart of the Theology of the Body. A vision that calls each of us to not only uphold but celebrate the indelible imprint of God in every human being.

Science and Faith in Human Uniqueness

The intricate dance between science and faith has long intrigued scholars and the faithful alike. When we consider what makes us uniquely human, we enter a sacred dialogue between these two realms. A synergy that invites us to explore how both contribute to understanding the human person as an image of God. It's a conversation that embraces both the empirical and the mystical, making space for believers to integrate and deepen their understanding of human nature.

At the core of faith, particularly within the Catholic tradition, lies the belief that humans are created in the image and likeness of God. This concept isn't merely a theological assertion; it's a foundational identity, setting individuals apart as bearers of divine dignity. Science, particularly in fields such as anthropology and biology, enriches this understanding by revealing the complexity and wonder of human evolution and development. Our genetic makeup, cognitive abilities, and capacity for language and abstract thought all speak to a remarkable uniqueness that stands out within creation.

Yet, more profound than our biological and cognitive traits is the spiritual dimension. The union of body and soul, as understood in Catholic teaching, sets humans apart in a way that's mysterious and magnificent. The soul doesn't diminish the role of the body; instead, it elevates it. Scientific inquiry into consciousness and neuroscience continues to pose profound questions about identity and the mind's relationship to the body, questions that echo the Church's exploration of the soul's reality.

In recent years, advancements in genetics and neuroscience have illuminated much about the human condition. These discoveries reveal a shared genetic heritage with other living beings, yet also highlight capabilities unique to humans. For instance, the complex moral reasoning, deep-seated sense of right and wrong, and the drive for justice and compassion—qualities not easily explained by genetics alone. These characteristics call for a deeper examination and invite a dialogue with theology, which provides context and meaning grounded in divine intention.

St. John Paul II, in his teachings on the Theology of the Body, encouraged us to see our bodies as communicating a truth that transcends physicality alone. Science can inform us about cells and synapses, giving us insight into our physical being, while faith speaks to our vocation to love and to seek communion with God and others. Together, they provide a fuller picture of what it means to be made in the "image of God."

Moreover, the integration of science and faith can inspire a deeper respect for life in all its stages and forms. The dignity of the human person is evident not just in our shared designs but in the way we choose to nurture, protect, and honor each life as a reflection of the divine. In this light, ethical questions, whether about life's beginning, end, or critical moments in between, are enriched by both scientific understanding and moral discernment rooted in faith.

The dialogue between science and faith is not without its challenges. Skeptics may argue that science has no need for the explanation of the divine, while some believers might worry that an over-reliance on scientific understanding could overshadow spiritual truths. However, history has shown time and again that complex challenges often invite collaboration rather than division. Let this dialogue be an encouragement for young people, Knights of Columbus, and educators forming the faithful to see beyond the apparent tensions and embrace the fullness of truth in every exploration.

Throughout history, many Catholic scientists and theologians have recognized this potential for harmony. Figures like Georges Lemaître, who proposed the Big Bang theory, remind us that scientific pursuit can exist alongside deep faith, each leading to a greater glorification of God's creation. They serve as role models for how faith can inspire scientific inquiry and how science can broaden the horizons of faith.

In teaching young adults and teenagers through a Theology of the Body curriculum, the aim should be to cultivate a sense of wonder and reverence for both the divine and the natural. It should encourage them to see their own bodies as sacred vessels, uniquely capable of reflecting God's presence in the world. Encouragement from mentors, like the Knights of Columbus, can guide them to navigate a world where scientific achievements and spiritual truths coexist.

Ultimately, an understanding of human uniqueness that embraces both science and faith leads to a more profound appreciation for the mystery of life and our role within it. It empowers us to face modern challenges with wisdom and compassion, to seek truth in all its forms, and to acknowledge the greatness of God in every facet of existence. The journey toward understanding ourselves as images of God is enriched by both our tangible and intangible dimensions, celebrated in a life of faith, hope, and love that responds to the divine call.

Chapter 4: Theology of Relationships

Theology of Relationships invites us to understand the profound bond designed by God, rooted in the essence of love and responsibility. This chapter encourages young people to see relationships as a sacred endeavor, a tangible reflection of God's divine communion. By learning to love authentically, we take part in an intimate dance that mirrors the Holy Trinity—each relationship bearing the potential to reveal His truth, beauty, and goodness. Grounded in empathy and wisdom, the Knights of Columbus offer guidance to help navigate the complexities of modern relationships, empowering young adults and teenagers to foster genuine connections that nurture both individual and communal holiness. It's about building healthy relationships where commitment, respect, and self-gift flourish, encouraging each one of us to see beyond ourselves, recognizing the inherent dignity in others as crafted in His image. As we engage with one another, we discover that love becomes not just an emotion but a conscious, life-giving act that aligns us more closely with our Creator's vision for humanity.

Love and Responsibility

In the heart of the Theology of Relationships lies the profound concept of "Love and Responsibility." This notion extends beyond mere emotional feeling or sentimentality, diving deep into the ethical and moral obligations that come with genuine love. These two intertwined elements—love and responsibility—form the cornerstone of how individuals are called to treat each other, respecting the inherent dignity of every person. The call is not merely to feel love but to act with love, positioning the good of the other as the primary concern, an idea that's both ancient and revolutionary.

The teachings of the Church, especially as articulated by Pope Saint John Paul II, emphasize that love is not just an abstract principle but a tangible force that requires duty, sacrifice, and accountability. He articulated that "true love," in its fullness, demands a complete and selfless gift of oneself, mirrored perfectly in the sacrificial love of Christ. By understanding and embracing this perspective, we gain a framework to navigate the complexities of relationships. It's a roadmap for fostering connections that are not only deep but also enduring, based on mutual respect and commitment.

Young adults and teenagers, the audience we focus on, often face a myriad of challenges when it comes to relationships. In a world saturated with fleeting connections and superficial interactions, the call to love responsibly offers a transformative perspective. It invites a re-evaluation of what it means to care for another person, urging a move away from transactional interactions to those rooted in genuine care and concern. Teenagers, particularly, must be guided to understand that true love isn't about exchanging benefits; it's about mutual growth and support.

Delving into the principle of responsibility within love means recognizing the power dynamics at play in every relationship. It's about acknowledging the influence one person holds over another and ensuring that such influence is wielded justly and compassionately. Responsibility here means being answerable not only to one's conscience but to God and the broader community. It emphasizes the need to act ethically and with integrity, ensuring that every action aligns with the higher calling of being the image of God's love to others.

The Knights of Columbus, in their mission, can play a pivotal role in advocating and embodying this principle among their communities. By fostering environments where both young people and adults are encouraged to reflect on their relationships through the lens of love and responsibility, they create spaces of growth and understanding. Programs and curricula can be developed that challenge participants to embody these ideas in practical and meaningful ways, promoting a culture that values ethical engagement and deep, abiding love.

It's crucial to remember that the framework of love and responsibility doesn't negate the natural human experience of love's complications and challenges. Instead, it provides a supportive structure to confront these issues head-on, equipped with a mindset that looks beyond the self. This approach can help dismantle the fear and hesitations that often accompany vulnerability in love. By fostering an understanding that responsibility is not a burden but a liberating force, individuals can approach relationships with greater joy and confidence.

In practical terms, living out love and responsibility can begin with small, everyday actions. It's about being present and attentive to others' needs, listening actively, and offering support without expecting anything in return. It's about standing by commitments, big or small, and recognizing the impact of one's words and actions. When this mindset is cultivated within young adults, it lays a foundation for long-lasting relationships—be they friendships, familial bonds, or romantic partnerships.

For teenagers in particular, it is crucial to understand this concept of love and responsibility as it relates to forming their own identity and understanding who they are in the eyes of God. It's an empowering realization that extends beyond oneself and taps into the interconnectedness of human relationships. The awareness that their actions and decisions can significantly affect others instills a sense of purpose and belonging.

Love and Responsibility also serve as a vital dialogue with contemporary challenges where relationships are concerned. Today's digital age presents unique dynamics in how people relate to one another. Many friendships and romantic connections are often formed and maintained online, where the immediacy and fleeting nature of interactions can sometimes mirror virtual "reality" more than genuine connection. Here, the principles of love and responsibility remind us of the importance of authenticity and real presence even when communication happens over digital platforms.

While navigating these realities, young Catholics are called to also discern the deeper purposes of their relationships through continuous prayer and reflection. Our faith offers numerous resources, such as the sacraments and Church teachings, that provide guidance and support on this journey. Participating in church activities and engaging with faith-based communities like the Knights of Columbus can reinforce these values, offering concrete examples and role models of living out this integrated love.

The journey of understanding and integrating love and responsibility within the theology of relationships is ongoing. It requires constant reflection, openness to growth, and an unwavering commitment to put these principles into action. With this foundation, our relationships can truly be transformative, mirroring the unconditional love that God offers to each of us and bringing about healing, growth, and connection in our lives.

In sum, the concept of Love and Responsibility within the Theology of Relationships calls us to a higher standard. It challenges us to love deeply, act ethically, and engage confidently with the world around us. It's a paradigm shift that has the power to transform not only our lives but also the communities we build together. As we embrace these principles, let us be continuous witnesses, shining examples of God's love in a world that desperately needs it.

Building Healthy Relationships

In a world where individualism often overshadows community, building healthy relationships takes on profound significance. This task aligns closely with the Theology of the Body, which challenges us to see relationships through the lens of divine love and unity. At the heart of this theology is the call to love selflessly, echoing the love that God has for humanity. Establishing relationships grounded in such love can transform not only personal connections but also communities and societies.

Healthy relationships don't just happen; they require active participation and intentionality. In the theology of relationships, we learn the importance of both giving and receiving in a balanced manner. It calls us to engage with one another through compassion, open communication, and forgiveness. These elements reflect the image of God's relational nature—Father, Son, and Holy Spirit—encouraging us to mirror unity within diversity.

Communication is the bedrock of any relationship. It involves more than just words; it encompasses the act of listening, understanding, and responding with empathy. Building healthy relationships means being present, not just physically but emotionally and spiritually. This attentiveness can often be challenging amidst the noise of modern life, but it's essential to cultivate moments of genuine connection, free from distractions, where true relational growth can occur.

Yet, communication alone isn't enough. A healthy relationship requires honesty and vulnerability. By being open about our strengths and weaknesses, joys and sorrows, we allow others to journey with us authentically. Such openness fosters trust and intimacy, laying a foundation where love can flourish unencumbered by pretense. These are not just human virtues but divine invitations to live in truth and connection.

Forgiveness is often viewed as a difficult path, yet it is indispensable in the journey of relationship-building. Theology of the Body teaches that forgiveness is more than a human gesture; it's a divine act that restores grace to fractured relationships. By forgiving, we participate in the redemptive love of Christ, transforming wounds into sources of grace and healing. This act doesn't deny the wrongs done but seeks to bring about reconciliation and peace.

Boundaries, paradoxically, also play a crucial role in building healthy relationships. They aren't barriers but guides that help manage personal space and autonomy while respecting others. Knowing and expressing personal boundaries can prevent potential conflicts and misunderstandings. This understanding promotes healthier interactions, ensuring that exchanges are driven by mutual respect and self-awareness.

Relational health also involves the commitment to work through difficulties rather than avoiding them. In a culture that sometimes prizes convenience, staying and resolving conflicts instead of fleeing is countercultural but deeply theological. Such commitment reflects God's unwavering covenant love, strengthening the bond between individuals and bringing them closer.

The journey of building healthy relationships also requires patience and grace. We all carry imperfections; hence, relationships will inevitably reflect human fallibility. Embracing an attitude of patient endurance, much like the saints we've grown to admire, can help us navigate these imperfections. Through patience, we create space for growth and transformation both in ourselves and others, nurturing an environment where holiness can take root.

Sacramental living deeply affects how we approach relationships. The sacraments are channels of divine grace that empower us to love more fully. In the Eucharist, we draw strength and nourishment to engage in love that sacrifices and serves. Moreover, through reconciliation, we're reminded of the power of renewal, continuously drawing us back to right relationship with God and each other. Participation in the sacraments fuels our capacity to live out the call to communion in practical ways.

Ephesians 4:2-3 serves as a guiding principle, urging us to conduct ourselves with humility, gentleness, and patience in relationships, striving to maintain the unity of the Spirit through the bond of peace. This scriptural foundation encourages us to reflect on our relational approaches and to align our interactions with the virtues of Christ himself. In striving for these ideals, relationships become avenues of divine encounter, where we can meet God in another.

The resilience found in living out a theology of relationships strengthens our communities and enriches our faith journey. As Knights of Columbus, young adults, and teenagers embrace these principles, they partake in a transformative mission that extends beyond themselves. They exemplify a lifestyle of love and communion, profoundly impacting the wider Church and world.

With intentionality, patience, and grace, we are called to invite God's love into our relationships. In this daily endeavor, we are not alone but supported by the community of saints, prayer, and the sacraments. What begins as personal growth ripples outward, contributing to a renewed understanding and experience of the Theology of the Body, lived out in the vibrant collage of human relationships.

Chapter 5: The Sacramentality of the Body

As we explore the meaning of the sacramentality of the body, we dive into a profound truth that connects our physical existence with the divine mysteries. This concept invites each of us to recognize our bodies not just as vessels but as sacred sites where God's love is unveiled. The body, in its unique articulation, becomes a reflection of the Creator, a temple housing the Holy Spirit meant to manifest holiness in everyday life. With each gesture, each interaction, our bodies hold the potential to communicate divine love and grace. Understanding this sacramental view compels us to embrace both the dignity and responsibility inherent in our bodily existence. Through this realization, teenagers and young adults within the Knights of Columbus are called to honor their bodies and others', fostering communities built on mutual respect and divine love. By anchoring themselves in these truths, they can lead lives that are not only enriched by faith but also exemplify a commitment to the sacredness intrinsic to human life. In this recognition, there's an ever-present invitation to look beyond the surface, seeing the inherent beauty and sanctity that our bodies reveal in the narrative of creation.

Body as a Temple

In the profound mystery of faith, the body is more than just a physical structure; it embodies a sacred gift. The Church teaches that we are the temple of the Holy Spirit, an intrinsic part of our very being. Recognizing this, the body becomes a vessel that carries divine significance, whispering a call to live in holiness and dignity. This sacred view of the body invites us to see ourselves and others as living manifestations of God's love and creativity.

When we say the body is a temple, the scriptural roots of this concept run deep. Saint Paul reminds us in his letters to the Corinthians that "your body is a temple of the Holy Spirit within you." This is not just a metaphor but a reality that asks us to treat our bodies with the care, respect, and reverence due to a holy edifice. As a temple houses the divine, so our bodies house our souls and the Spirit, intertwining our physical actions with spiritual grace.

Historically, temples have been places of gathering, prayer, and communion with the divine. In this light, understanding the body as a temple prompts us to reflect on how we use our bodies in the daily overture of life. It's a prompt to examine: Do our actions weave threads of harmony, kindness, and love? Or do we sometimes falter, allowing traits less becoming of a temple to slip through? This reflection is vital in aligning our bodily actions with the holy mission we are called to fulfill.

For young Catholics and members of the Knights of Columbus, recognizing the sacrality of the body provides a guiding compass. In a world often challenging traditional values, understanding that our bodies echo a higher purpose can be an anchor. It can shape how we see ourselves and others, fostering a community where every person is respected as part of God's magnificent creation. This awareness can be transformational, helping young adults and teenagers navigate identity and peer pressure.

Celebrating the body as a temple inevitably leads us to consider how we care for this divine dwelling. This care extends beyond physical health, though that's certainly important, to encompass our mental and spiritual wellness. Honor your body by nourishing it with good food, regular exercise, and sufficient rest. Yet, equally significant is nurturing your mind with truth and your soul with prayer. This holistic approach echoes the Church's teaching that care for your body is inseparable from care for your soul.

The Knights of Columbus can play a pivotal role here, guiding young members in understanding and embodying this sacramental vision. Through workshops, discussions, and personal mentoring, they can instill values that elevate the perception of the body from commonplace to consecrated. Such guidance can help youth internalize the significance of living in a way that respects their intrinsic sanctity, which is especially pertinent in today's media-driven culture, often intent on mocking or diminishing spiritual truths.

Having a body demands responsibility. The concept of the body as a temple invites us not only to reflect on ourselves but also to serve others through acts of kindness and compassion. The physical becomes a means to uphold spiritual virtues. Carrying groceries for an elderly person, volunteering, offering a shoulder to cry on—these everyday acts of service are ways our bodies manifest divine love. They become testaments of faithful stewardship, showing that we value our God-given role in creation.

Understanding our bodies as sacred can be invigorating for the imagination, inspiring us to create environments where such truths are recognized and lived out. In parish communities, youth ministries, and Knights of Columbus councils, this belief can revitalize how we practice our faith. By honoring and respecting our bodies, we cultivate spaces where grace and humanity flourish hand in hand.

Furthermore, the analogy of the body as a temple encourages us to seek healing and forgiveness when we fall short of this divine ideal. God's mercy is an endless well, and recognizing our bodies as holy makes room for receiving this mercy. Confession and reconciliation offer us paths to renew the temple when sin may have tarnished its beauty. These sacraments provide us the strength to rise again, just as Christ rose, restoring the grandeur of the temples we are called to be.

Finally, seeing the body as a temple prompts a transformative worldview. It's a call to rise above societal pressures that may devalue human life or the sanctity of the body. It's an invitation to join with others in building a culture of life, understanding, and dignity. This calling pulsates with hope and challenges young people to swim against the tide of a culture often disinterested in or hostile to spiritual truths. Accepting this mission is no easy feat, but it is a journey worth undertaking.

In living our lives with the understanding that the body is a temple, we leave a legacy of faith, one that can inspire future generations. We bear witness to the truth woven into the fabric of our humanity—that each of us is a beloved temple of the Holy Spirit. Let us embrace this reality with joy, courage, and steadfast commitment to the ideals that enrich our lives and our community as Knights of Columbus and faithful followers of Christ.

Holiness Manifested in the Body

Holiness isn't just an abstract concept reserved for the spiritually elite. It's something real and tangible, meant for each of us, and it finds profound expression in our bodies. The idea that our bodies can be vessels of holiness might be challenging at first. We live in a world that often separates the sacred from the physical, treating them as if they're incompatible. However, in God's design, the body isn't merely a shell or an obstacle to be overcome on the path to sanctity. Instead, it's integral to our spiritual journey. Our bodies are gifts through which we experience, express, and reflect holiness in our daily lives.

The body serves as a "temple of the Holy Spirit," as Saint Paul reminds us in his letters. This scriptural insight sheds light on how we are living tabernacles of God's presence. Everything we do—every action, every word—comes from this hallowed vessel, which is sacred and dignified by its very nature. Our daily interactions, such as a kind gesture or a heartfelt conversation, offer opportunities for holiness to be made visible through our physical presence. It's in these ordinary moments that our bodies become living icons of God's kindness and love in the world.

Consider how simple, human processes—such as breathing, eating, or walking—are imbued with opportunities for sanctity. When done with mindfulness and gratitude, even these mundane acts become participations in the divine. Here lies the joy of recognizing God's hand in the rhythms of everyday life. For young adults and teenagers, this perception can infuse their routines with purpose. It's an invitation to understand that there's no aspect of life too trivial or ordinary to reflect God's glory.

The body is not just a personal artifact; it's a shared part of our communal life. When we extend a helping hand to those in need, when we partake in sacraments like the Eucharist, or even when we simply listen with compassion, we enact a form of service that sanctifies our bodies. This communal aspect highlights that holiness isn't for isolation but for the flourishing of the whole body of Christ. In giving and receiving the support of community, we live out our vocation of love, enriching our bodily experience with shared purpose and grace.

Developing an understanding of holiness in the body reshapes our view of self-discipline and sacrifice. Far from being mere denial or austerity, it's about aligning our physical actions with the love and sacrifice of Christ. It's where diet, exercise, and rest become more than health concerns—they turn into practices of stewardship over the gift that each body represents. Choosing to respect the sacredness of our bodies means embracing lifestyles that reject excess, unhealthy habits, or anything that hinders our closeness to God.

This perspective on bodily holiness provides a robust framework for approaching the life choices young adults and Knights of Columbus face. As custodians of this divine manifestation, the call goes beyond the personal, extending into how we engage with modern culture's views on the body. In a society where body image can often lead to anxiety and disconnection, understanding the body as a manifestation of holiness offers a transformative lens through which to see oneself and others.

Fostering this awareness calls for a heart that sees the interconnection between spirit and body. It involves cultivating gratitude and reverence for the body in daily life. Recognizing its divine imprint helps to combat the objectification and commodification that is rampant today. Instead of viewing the body as an object of superficial judgment, it becomes a testament to God's love, creativity, and boundless grace.

Our bodies also have a liturgical dimension that celebrates God's ongoing work in our lives. Through gestures of prayer and worship—standing, kneeling, Bowing—we participate in a dance of sacred movement, expressing the inner truth of our faith. It's here, in the sacred rhythm of liturgy, where the holiness of our bodies finds its fullest expression, as every motion becomes a proclamation of God's beauty and holiness.

Achieving a deeper understanding of how our bodies reflect holiness is a lifelong journey, one that requires thoughtful reflection, education, and community support. By incorporating insights from theology, liturgical practices, and personal prayer, Knights of Columbus can lead by example, guiding young adults and teenagers in recognizing their bodies as temples of sanctity made for God's glory. This endeavor involves both learning and lived experience, fostering a pathway that integrates faith and life harmoniously.

Ultimately, holiness in the body is an invitation to see the ordinary with extraordinary eyes, knowing that through our bodies, we possess the capacity to reveal God's presence. As Knights, committed to fostering a culture of life, there's an imperative to support and encourage this understanding within our communities. By lifting each other up in this endeavor, the Knights can empower the youth to embrace their true identity as God's beloved, whose bodies, indeed, have the capacity to manifest holiness in the world.

Chapter 6: The Vocation to Love

In the heart of our journey through the Theology of the Body, we arrive at an exploration of the deepest calling etched into every human soul: the vocation to love. As Roman Catholics and members of the Knights of Columbus, young adults and teenagers are invited to discern this universal calling — whether it unfolds through marriage, religious life, or a dedicated single life. By engaging with this vocation, we acknowledge love as more than an emotion; it is a guiding, transformative force that mirrors the divine love God extends to humanity. Our challenge, then, is to open our hearts to the myriad ways this vocation can manifest, embracing the humility and courage needed to follow a path illuminated by faith. Let us embrace this call with compassion and responsibility, recognizing that our choices and actions in love shape not only our destinies but also the community and world around us.

Different Vocations in Life

In the grand tapestry of life, each thread represents a unique calling, a vocation meant to weave into a larger picture filled with love, purpose, and divine intention. The vocation to love, as envisioned by "Theology of the Body," is not a one-size-fits-all mandate. Instead, it welcomes an array of paths, allowing every person to discern and embrace their unique role in the world. This understanding invites us to see vocations not just as jobs or roles, but as the very essence of how we embody love in our lives.

For many, the vocation to married life stands out as a prominent path, forming the foundation for family and community. It's a shared journey where two individuals become one in purpose, reflecting the covenantal love of Christ and His Church. Marriage is not merely a social contract but a divine calling to love and to foster new life, becoming a visible sign of God's unending love. It's in the daily gestures, the shared dreams, and even the trials, that this vocation finds its deepest expression. The family home becomes a "domestic church," a place where virtues are taught, love is lived, and faith is nurtured.

Then there's the single life, often misunderstood as a waiting room for something more, but in reality, it's a vocation rich with its own purpose. Singleness can be a call to dedicate one's energy, time, and love to community service, professional growth, or personal spiritual development. It's a path that allows for unique contributions to society and the Church that are equally vital and cherished. Those who live out this vocation find freedom in their commitment — a freedom that allows them to serve with a wholehearted love, echoing St. Paul's encouragement to undivided devotion to the Lord.

In some hearts, the vocation to religious life or ordained ministry echoes as a clear, undeniable call. Priests, monks, nuns, and those in consecrated life dedicate themselves to God and His Church in an intimacy that mirrors Christ's own life. Through vows of poverty, chastity, and obedience, these individuals live in community and prayer, serving as beacons of God's love and committing their lives to the spiritual welfare of others. This vocation is a profound expression of love, as it requires a self-giving that is complete, surrendering personal desires for the greater needs of the body of Christ.

Regardless of which path is chosen, each vocation requires discernment — a prayerful process of listening to God's voice in one's heart and in the circumstances of life. It's about engaging with the divine and asking, "How am I called to love in a way that is uniquely mine?" Discerning one's vocation is not just a decision-making process but a spiritual journey that requires patience, openness, and trust in the Holy Spirit's guidance.

As young Catholics, particularly members of the Knights of Columbus, approach this stage of discerning their vocations, they're supported by a rich tradition of community and faith. The Knights, with their commitment to charity, unity, fraternity, and patriotism, offer a framework that encourages young adults to explore these vocations within a supportive brotherhood. By understanding their personal vocation as a call to love, young members are equipped to transform their understanding of self and community, becoming active participants in the mission of the Church.

Ultimately, the vocation to love is at the heart of every calling. Whether through marriage, single life, religious consecration, or ordained ministry, it's about living out the image of God within us. By choosing a vocation that aligns with our deepest, truest selves, we honor that divine image and contribute to the world as instruments of God's love. In navigating these different vocations, we find not only personal fulfillment but also the joy of building up the body of Christ in all its diverse expressions.

Embracing this vocation is a testament to faith, a leap into a life of purpose that transcends personal ambition to weave a legacy of love. It's a journey that continually calls for renewal and growth, inviting each of us to ask, "How am I expressing love today?" By staying true to this call, we find ourselves not just fulfilling a role, but carving out a path that leads to deeper communion with God and with others.

Discerning One's Path

As we journey through life, each of us is invited to discern how best we can live out our vocation to love. This isn't just about finding a career or choosing a lifestyle; it's about understanding the unique path that God calls us to undertake. This path is where our deepest desires meet the world's greatest needs, and where our lives become the embodiment of love's transformative power.

Discerning one's path requires attentive listening to God's voice. In a world filled with noise and distractions, tuning into the divine whisper can be challenging. Yet, this quiet voice holds the blueprint for a life of purpose and fulfillment. Consider the tools we have at our disposal: prayer, community, and the sacraments. Each acts as a spiritual compass, pointing us toward the path of authentic love and meaningful existence.

Prayer is where our discernment often begins. It is a dialogue with God, one where we can lay our questions and desires at His feet. Through prayer, we learn to hear the subtle nudges of the Holy Spirit guiding us in our decisions. The silence of a prayerful heart allows God's voice to rise above the chaos, offering clarity amid confusion.

However, discernment doesn't occur in solitude. We find guidance in the Church community, a gathering of hearts and minds seeking the same divine direction. The support of others provides insight and accountability, rooting us in a shared journey toward Christ. Within this community, mentors and examples inspire us, showing that the path we seek isn't just theoretical—it's lived, day by day, in loving acts and service.

The sacraments serve as touchpoints in our journey, where God's grace nourishes our soul. In the Eucharist, we find strength; in Reconciliation, forgiveness and renewal. Each sacrament is a reminder of the divine love that calls us forward, urging us to become who we are meant to be. They are anchors, ensuring we remain in His love while searching for our vocation.

Recognizing one's vocation is about aligning personal talents and passions with God's plan. Every person possesses unique gifts, and our challenge lies in discovering how these can glorify God and serve others. Whether called to married life, religious vocation, or single life, each path is equally dignified and necessary in the unfolding of God's kingdom.

In practical terms, discerning one's path means stepping out in faith, even when the way isn't clear. It involves embracing uncertainty with courage, trusting that God's vision for us is good—even when it asks us to venture beyond our comfort zones. Life's decisions become opportunities to express love as a dynamic, active force that shapes our world.

In the discernment process, patience is a virtue to cultivate. God's timing may not align with our schedules, but it's always perfect. Learning to wait without anxiety, to rest in the assurance of Divine Providence, strengthens faith and deepens our trust in the journey we are on. This patience cultivates a peace that guards our hearts and minds as we make choices aligned with His will.

There's humility, too, in recognizing that our path may not be straightforward or without obstacles. Embracing the twists and turns with grace reflects our understanding that God's ways are not our ways. Life's detours often become transformative experiences, teaching us lessons that pave the way for a richer and more fulfilling vocation.

The process of discerning one's path is not a solitary endeavor but a shared pilgrimage. Walking with others who are similarly seeking God's direction enriches our journey. The Knights of Columbus offer a brotherhood that fosters the values of charity, unity, and fraternity—values that align perfectly with the call to love in all vocations. Within this brotherhood, young adults and teenagers find worthwhile companions in spiritual and personal growth.

Ultimately, discerning one's path is about discovering our place in God's story—a narrative woven with love from beginning to end. It's where we learn that our vocation is not merely about doing but being. Being loved by God, and being a conduit of His love to the world. This is the divine invitation extended to us all.

As you navigate this journey of discerning your vocation, remember that God is always near, offering guidance and love as you step into your unique role in His divine plan. Embrace the uncertainties with a heart full of faith, and you will surely find the path that leads to a life filled with purpose and peace.

Chapter 7: Marriage and Family

In our journey through life, marriage and family stand as cornerstones, reflecting the divine blueprint of love and communion. They're not merely social constructs; they are sacred covenants rooted in the self-giving love modeled by Christ Himself. In the sacrament of marriage, man and woman become partners bound by a promise that reflects the unity of the Trinity, offering themselves wholly and unreservedly. Family, in its essence, is a nurturing ground where virtues are sown and the seeds of faith are cultivated. Each family faces challenges, yet through grace, these trials transform into opportunities for growth and deeper connection. By embracing the theology of family life, young Catholics can navigate these complexities with courage and fidelity, drawing on the rich tradition and wisdom of the Church. Here lies the cradle where future generations are formed, a domestic church where love is both taught and lived.

Theology of Family Life

In the grand narrative of human existence, family life holds a unique and sacred place. When we explore the theology of family life, we dive into a profound understanding of our connection to God and one another. It's in family that we first learn about love, sacrifice, and communion, mirroring the divine relationship within the Holy Trinity.

The family is often referred to as the "domestic church," a term emphasizing its critical role in nurturing faith and cultivating virtues. This idea isn't just a catchy phrase—it's a truth embedded in the teachings of the Church. Each family is called to embody the love of Christ, becoming a beacon of God's light in an often darkened world.

Our appreciation for family life is deeply rooted in Scripture. The Bible teems with examples of familial relationships, from the very first family of Adam and Eve to the Holy Family of Jesus, Mary, and Joseph. These stories offer us a kaleidoscope f lessons, showing us the joys and challenges of family life. They remind us that even in imperfection, there is grace and the possibility for holiness.

Love within the family is not a passive endeavor. It requires an active commitment to put others before oneself, mirroring the sacrificial love that Christ demonstrated on the cross. This kind of love, agape, is self-giving and unconditional. It's the foundation upon which a healthy family is built, fostering an environment where each member can grow towards their God-given potential.

The theology of family life also emphasizes the sanctity of marriage, which serves as its cornerstone. In marriage, a husband and wife participate in a sacred covenant, reflecting the everlasting covenant between Christ and His Church. This union transcends the personal, bearing a communal and even cosmic significance. The marital bond is life-giving, oriented towards the creation and nurturing of new life, echoing the creative love of God.

Parenting, too, is an expression of this theology. It's more than just raising children; it's a divine vocation to lead these souls toward their ultimate destiny in Christ. Parents are the first educators in the faith, tasked with guiding their children not only by words but through the powerful witness of their own lives. The home becomes the first arena of evangelization, a place where the young learn to cherish the teachings of the Church, embrace its morals, and live them out daily.

However, we must acknowledge the challenges that families face in modern society. The distractions and pressures of contemporary life can stretch family bonds thin and obscure their divine purpose. Economic strains, societal expectations, and the rapid pace of technological change all play their part in this equation. Yet, it is precisely through these difficulties that grace abounds, calling families to rely not solely on their strengths but on God's unwavering support.

The role of the extended family, godparents, and the wider faith community cannot be underestimated. They offer support, wisdom, and encouragement, helping families carry out their spiritual mission. This network of relationships strengthens the core unit of the family, acting as a bulwark against the challenges each family faces.

In this theological vision, every family is called to be a place of prayer. Regular family prayer creates a rhythm of grace, centering the family's life on God. Whether it's the simple practice of grace before meals or a family rosary, these moments stitch divine threads into the family's daily fabric, reminding everyone of their ultimate purpose and guide.

As families strive to live out this divine calling, they become symbols to the world of what is possible through God's grace. They reflect the joy, commitment, and tenacity that love demands. They amplify the message of Christ's unconditional love, offering hope in a world that desperately needs it.

The Knights of Columbus can play a pivotal role in promoting and supporting this vision. As part of their mission, they uphold the sanctity of family life, offering resources, community support, and prayerful solidarity. Together, as a united body in Christ, families and the Knights of Columbus can stand as a testament to the beauty and challenge of the theology of family life.

In summary, the theology of family life isn't simply an ideal to strive towards—it's a lived reality that demands our participation, intent, and openness to God's transforming power. By embracing this call, families become sanctuaries of love and faith, each unique but connected in the grand story of redemption. The work is demanding but immeasurably rewarding, echoing the eternal promise of joy and fulfillment found in communion with God and one another.

Challenges and Grace in Family

Family life - a beautiful quilt woven with love, tradition, and faith. Yet, as anyone who's part of a family knows, it's not without its tangles and trials. Embracing the familial journey means confronting both the joys and the struggles that life presents. For Roman Catholics, the family isn't just a social institution; it is the domestic church, a sacred ground where the faith is lived and passed on like a cherished heirloom. This calling underscores the importance of nurturing both the spiritual and emotional facets of family life, amidst challenges ranging from interpersonal conflicts to societal pressures.

Living in modern times brings unique challenges to families. Technology, while a tool for connection, also presents distractions that can intrude on family time. The hustle and bustle of daily life, pulling family members in multiple directions, often leaves little room for shared experiences and prayer. Yet, it's precisely within these challenges that grace abounds. The family, relying on the steadfastness of faith, learns to navigate through crises, bolstered by prayer, patience, and an unwavering commitment to each member's well-being.

In reflecting on these challenges, it's crucial to recognize the grace that permeates family life. Every obstacle encountered becomes an opportunity for growth—not merely in personal virtues but collectively as a family unit. During times of conflict, whether it's a difference of opinion or deeper misunderstandings, patience and forgiveness serve as guiding lights. Catholic teachings underscore the transformative power of these virtues, which enable family members to reconcile and renew their bonds. Such instances of grace not only fortify individual hearts but also envelope the entire family in a profound sense of unity.

The sacrament of marriage, a cornerstone of family life, offers a profound illustration of how challenges and grace interweave. In marriage, two individuals embark on a lifelong journey of love and sacrifice, mirroring Christ's love for the Church. This covenant is continuously tested through life's unpredictability, yet upheld by grace derived from prayer, the sacraments, and a shared commitment to fostering a domestic church. Marriage demands communication, openness, and a willingness to grow together through hardship, recognizing that each challenge is a stepping stone toward a deeper, more holy union.

Children bring a different dynamic, redefining the family structure and amplifying joy and responsibility. Parenting requires an openness to grace, asking parents to foster an environment where love, discipline, and faith complement each other. As children mature, parents face the challenge of guiding them through life's complexities, using the wisdom of Catholic teachings as both shield and sword. It's a journey of constant learning, growth, and reliance on divine grace to instill faith and virtues in the next generation.

Furthermore, the family doesn't exist in isolation. Communities—both parish and secular—have a significant impact on family life. Social pressures, cultural shifts, and even political climates can influence familial values and priorities. A Roman Catholic family, immersed in faith, draws strength from church communities, participating in liturgical celebrations, and sharing in parish life. This communal participation offers a supportive network that helps families stay grounded in faith, even when external challenges arise.

While societal changes present hurdles, they also offer opportunities for families to witness the Gospel in new, dynamic ways. An active, faith-filled family becomes a beacon of light and hope, showcasing the power and presence of grace in everyday life. By living out their faith, families not only strengthen their own bonds but also become testimonies to the wider community, promoting values of love, justice, and mercy.

It's in the simple daily acts that grace is most visible. Whether it's setting aside time for family prayer, sharing meals, celebrating the sacraments together, or offering support in times of need, these moments accumulate to create a system of holiness. Recognizing Christ in one another and embracing each member's uniqueness, the family fulfills its vocation as a reflection of the divine community of love.

Ultimately, while the path of family life is fraught with challenges, it's also traversed by God's abundant grace. Each family, though unique in its composition and experiences, shares the universal call to holiness. By embracing this call, supported by faith and the sacraments, families navigate through struggles with hope, resilience, and unyielding love. Through grace, families not only survive amidst challenges; they thrive, illuminating their homes and the world with the enduring light of Christ.

Chapter 8: Chastity and Its Importance

Chastity is more than abstaining from physical intimacy outside the bonds of sacramental marriage; it's a virtue that calls us to integrate our sexuality with our spiritual lives. This integration fosters respect for the dignity of ourselves and others, seeing each person as a beloved child of God rather than objects to be used. For Roman Catholics, particularly young adults and teens, chastity offers a path to genuine freedom—liberating one's heart to love authentically and selflessly. The Knights of Columbus echo this through their commitment to nurturing a Theology of the Body curriculum that helps form hearts and minds. Chastity, when embraced, acts like a shield against the distorted views of love pervasive in today's culture, guiding the faithful towards relationships grounded in truth and mutual respect. This virtue acts as a cornerstone for all vocations, safeguarding the sanctity of marriage and family, and preparing individuals for a life of abundant love. By living a chaste life, we open ourselves to experience the profound joy and peace that comes from living in harmony with God's purpose for our bodies and souls.

Understanding Chastity

Chastity may often be misunderstood, particularly in today's fast-paced and ever-changing world. It's vital, though, to grasp its true meaning within the framework of our faith. Deeply rooted in the teachings of the Church, chastity isn't merely the act of celibacy or avoidance of sexual relations outside marriage. It represents a broader, richer concept of purity and devotion that reaches into every facet of our lives. Chastity calls upon us to honor our bodies and those of others through love that's authentic and selfless.

In the context of Catholic teaching, chastity is one of the cardinal virtues. It forms a bridge between our earthly lives and the divine love God desires for us. It's about integrating our sexuality into our lives in a way that's full of dignity and respect. In a sense, chastity frees us from the selfishness that can come with distorted passions. It opens a path to genuine relationships, where we see others not as objects of desire but as beloved children of God.

This virtue challenges people of all walks—whether we're single, married, or consecrated to religious life. The Knights of Columbus have long understood this, recognizing chastity as central to their mission of building a civilization founded on love and truth. By placing chastity in the heart of their educational programs and communal activities, they promote a culture that respects life and helps young adults navigate relationships with integrity and respect.

But how do we cultivate chastity in our own lives, amidst the turbulence of emotions and societal pressures? Pope Saint John Paul II, in his Theology of the Body, emphasized the need for a personal commitment to understanding our bodies not merely as physical entities but as spiritual beings capable of divine goodness. Chastity, therefore, requires ongoing self-discipline, prayer, and education. It's a journey—an ongoing conversation with God—inviting us to constantly align our desires with His will.

For teenagers and young adults navigating their formative years, chastity can be a powerful, defining choice. It's not just about avoiding sin, but actively choosing a lifestyle that respects the self and others. By practicing chastity, young people learn about true love, which encompasses gift, responsibility, and sacrifice. They gain wisdom that surpasses fleeting passions and grasp the profound joy in channeling their energies towards fulfilling relationships and life goals.

The rapid spread of technology and shifting cultural norms often present unique challenges to living a chaste life. Yet, understanding chastity empowers young people to use technology responsibly, avoiding content that objectifies and degrades the dignity of the human person. It teaches discernment, encouraging individuals to cultivate interactions that reflect purity and kindness, both on and offline.

Chastity aligns beautifully with the teachings on the body as a temple, introduced earlier in our discussion. It's through this lens that we can understand our bodies as sacred places where God dwells. By remaining chaste, we honor this divine abode, recognizing that our value isn't hinged merely on physical attractiveness or romantic conquests but on our deeper, inherent worth as God's children.

Interestingly, chastity isn't a call to repression but to authentic freedom. It liberates us from the chains of lust and enables us to experience love in its fullness. In striving for a chaste heart, we're encouraged to foster genuine affection and compassion for one another, living out the call to love that Jesus exemplified and taught his disciples.

This journey isn't without its struggles and trials. Yet, these challenges are not insurmountable. With the right support, be it community, mentors from the Knights of Columbus, or spiritual guidance, each of us can strengthen our resolve. Holy scripture and the writings of the saints also provide rich resources and reflections that inspire and fortify our commitment to live chastely.

Ultimately, chastity is about aligning our heart's desires with the heart of God. It's a wholehearted yes to love's true nature, which is patient, kind, and not self-seeking. Through understanding chastity, we're invited to embrace a life that's vibrant, full of meaning and directed toward the horizon of our ultimate calling in God's eternal embrace.

Living a Chaste Life

Living a chaste life isn't just about renouncing certain behaviors. It's a profound commitment to seeing our bodies, relationships, and desires through the lens of God's love. Chastity invites us to honor the dignity inherent in ourselves and others, an idea deeply rooted in the Theology of the Body. It's a path to freedom, contrary to misunderstandings that might portray it as restrictive. Instead, chastity opens a space for true love to flourish, unencumbered by objectification or lust.

Chastity calls us to a higher understanding of love, where giving oneself doesn't rely on the fleeting passions of the moment but on a lasting dedication to the good of another. This journey integrates our physical desires with our spiritual convictions, creating harmony rather than conflict. Many young Catholics, including members of the Knights of Columbus, are on this journey, seeking to understand and live out this aspect of their faith in a world that often presents contrasting messages.

The starting point for living a chaste life is to acknowledge the value of self-control. In a culture that often glorifies immediate gratification, self-discipline becomes a radical, almost counter-cultural statement. It requires patience and perseverance, virtues that build strength and resilience in our moral character. By training ourselves to be masters of our desires rather than slaves to them, we grow in freedom and authenticity. This mastery enriches all our relationships, allowing us to love without seeking anything in return.

Chastity isn't a one-size-fits-all concept but discerned uniquely in different vocations, whether one is single, married, or consecrated. For teenagers and young adults, this means cultivating a respectful understanding of courtship. Dating becomes a dance of discovery and respect, not just a pursuit of pleasure. The Knights of Columbus can guide young members through mentorship, offering a model of living that balances virtue with grace.

We must also address the role of the modern world in our understanding and live out of chastity. With pervasive exposure to media and technology, young people are often bombarded with contrary ideals. The pressure to conform to cultural norms that devalue chastity is immense. Yet, here lies an opportunity to reshape these narratives, drawing from the beauty of our faith to present an alternative that resonates with authenticity and depth. It's about being intentional in the media we consume and mindful of the messages we internalize.

Moreover, living chaste lives is not to ignore our sexuality but to celebrate it in its full dignity. Our bodies are temples of the Holy Spirit, meant to radiate God's glory through love that is self-giving and pure. Such a life respects the sacredness of what it means to be human and reflects the divine image imprinted on each person. This respect transforms how we view ourselves and others, fostering environments of mutual honor and integrity.

A supportive community is crucial in this journey. The Knights of Columbus, along with parish communities, can foster environments that nurture this vision of chastity. Building such communities involves open conversations that dispel myths, address challenges, and share testimonies of living out this virtue joyfully. These spaces allow individuals to ask questions, seek guidance, and receive encouragement.

The sacramental life, especially frequent participation in the Eucharist and Reconciliation, supports living a chaste life. The sacraments provide grace that strengthens us against temptation and purifies our intentions. Through confession, we acknowledge where we've strayed and receive the grace necessary to begin anew—restored and ready to renew our commitment to chastity.

For young Catholics, role models are essential in this walk. Seeing peers and mentors living authentically as chaste individuals communicates that this lifestyle, though challenging, is attainable and fulfilling. Role models can illustrate how chastity is not just a personal decision but a social commitment, promoting a culture of life that recognizes and treasures human dignity at every stage.

Another aspect of living a chaste life is appreciating the positive impact it has on mental and emotional well-being. Chastity encourages honesty, transparency, and genuine intimacy in relationships. By aligning our actions with our values, we find a peace that permeates our lives, counteracting the anxiety that arises from living in duplicity. There's a joy found in the simple purity of heart and the clarity it brings to our interactions.

In conclusion, living a chaste life is a journey that requires dedication, patience, and an ongoing engagement with God's grace. For young members of the Catholic community and the Knights of Columbus, it's about embracing chastity as a pathway that enriches their spiritual, emotional, and relational lives. It's not merely about rules but about nurturing a heart capable of genuine love, a love that reflects the beauty and truth of the divine. Through community, sacramental support, and the cultivation of virtues, one can find the strength to live out this calling, shaping a life that truly embodies the joy and freedom of Christ-centered love.

Chapter 9: Theology of the Body in Daily Life

Living out the Theology of the Body each day is about seeing with the eyes of faith, where every moment becomes an opportunity to encounter the divine. Whether in a bustling classroom, a serene chapel, or around the family dinner table, the call is to recognize the sacred worth and dignity imprinted on each body by God Himself. Embracing this theology practically means more than understanding it intellectually—it involves letting it transform how we perceive and interact with others. As Knights of Columbus and fellow believers, we aspire to cultivate spaces where love and authenticity flourish, bearing witness to a world often lured by superficial values. Consider how the grace-filled stewardship of our bodies and relationships becomes a testament to our Creator, bridging the profound with the ordinary through simple acts of kindness, patience, and earnest conversation. In doing so, we knit a tapestry of community that honors God's presence in every heartbeat, making His love tangible and inviting others to discover the divine reality of their own lives. By consciously integrating this theology into small daily interactions, we gradually craft lives that mirror divine wisdom, peppered with the humble yet profound joy of knowing we are beloved in this grand story authored by God.

Practical Examples

Theology of the Body isn't just a concept to explore in a classroom or a church. It's a way of living that unfolds daily through conscious acts, choices, and relationships. For young adults, integrating these ideas into everyday life can be transformative. Let's delve into some practical examples of how Theology of the Body can be embodied and lived out each day.

Consider how you start your day. The moment your feet hit the floor in the morning is an opportunity to offer your day to God. It might seem insignificant, but this simple act of intention can shape your entire mindset. Whether you're heading to school, work, or fulfilling other responsibilities, this mindful beginning can reaffirm your role as an image of God. This isn't merely about maintaining outward piety but recognizing that our bodies, in all their actions, are temples meant for glorifying God.

In relationships, particularly friendships, Theology of the Body calls us to see beyond superficial interactions. Friendships rooted in this theology are not mere conveniences or emotional attachments; they're commitments to see the other person as Christ sees them. This might manifest in listening more deeply, offering help without expecting anything in return, or just being present during times of joy and sorrow. Young people can initiate faith-based group discussions where themes of love, respect, and responsibility can be explored and lived together, deepening communal bonds.

For young people, technology and social media are integral parts of daily life. How does Theology of the Body guide interactions in these spaces? Every message, every image shared, should reflect the dignity and respect that this theology upholds. It calls for authenticity and truth-telling, combating the culture of comparison and judgment rampant online. Knights of Columbus youth groups can organize workshops on responsible digital citizenship, illustrating how to post, tweet, and comment in ways that uplift rather than diminish the divine image within each person.

The call to chastity often intersects with daily life in subtle yet profound ways. It's not simply about abstaining from certain behaviors but embracing a holistic view of love that honors the self and others. Young people can embody this by setting healthy boundaries in their relationships, focusing on self-control, and pursuing emotional and spiritual purity. This could mean choosing to have conversations encouraging mutual growth rather than getting involved in gossip or harmful talk.

Understanding that the body is a gift compels a shift in how we care for ourselves. This isn't limited to spiritual or moral purity but extends to physical health and well-being. Encouraging daily exercise, healthy eating, and enough rest can be seen as acts of love and respect for the temple of the Holy Spirit. Knights of Columbus members might promote fitness challenges within their communities, intertwining physical activity with spiritual reflections on the temple of the body.

Community service offers another context for living out Theology of the Body. Volunteering isn't merely about completing a task or earning community service hours; it's an embodiment of self-giving love. Simple acts of kindness like helping a neighbor, participating in food drives, or supporting local charities are tangible ways to express this theology. These acts honor the interconnectedness of all people, challenging young and old alike to transcend self-interest for the greater good.

The concept of vocation is pivotal in daily applications of Theology of the Body. Even for teenagers and young adults, understanding one's vocation, whether it leads to religious life, marriage, or a single life dedicated to service, is crucial. Engaging in soul-searching conversations, attending retreats, or seeking guidance from mentors can help individuals discern their paths. This ongoing discernment underlines daily decisions and actions, encouraging a life aligned with one's divine calling.

Finally, engaging in the arts can beautifully express Theology of the Body. Art, whether it's music, dance, painting, or theatre, offers a medium to explore and express the divine intricacies of the human form and spirit. Organizing or participating in events that celebrate sacred art can inspire a deeper appreciation of the body as a reflection of God's creativity. By painting a mural with a community or writing a poem about creation, one can manifest the core principles of this theology through creativity.

Incorporating Theology of the Body into daily life requires intention and mindfulness, recognizing that every action, no matter how small, can reflect divine love. As these examples illustrate, it's about viewing life through a lens that sees the holiness in ordinary moments and understanding our call to love and dignity. This integration into daily practices not only enriches personal spirituality but also radiates outward, transforming the world one interaction at a time.

Embracing the Theology

Integrating the gift of the Theology of the Body into daily life is not just about understanding it intellectually but living it out in a palpable way. In every encounter, the call to live this theology manifests itself in the choices we make—as individuals, as families, and as communities. This journey drives us to respect the incredible dignity in each person we meet, recognizing that our own bodies are sacred spaces meant to reflect divine love. This focus fosters a shift from a self-centric view to one deeply rooted in love and authentic connection.

To truly embrace the Theology of the Body, it's essential that each of us first cultivates a lifestyle that sees the body not merely as a physical form, but as a profound medium of God's grace. This perspective invites us to realize that our bodies are a living testament to God's covenant with humanity.

Thus, every action, conversation, and decision becomes an opportunity to reflect God's presence in the world. Rather than being ideals that are unreachable, these concepts are practical—and impatient, awaiting to shape our day-to-day interactions.

Take, for instance, the way we choose to present ourselves. Are our clothing and demeanor expressions of the dignity that we, and everyone else, inherently possess as images of God? In embracing this theology, there is a call to authenticity—an outward harmony that reflects the inner reality of our communion with God.

For young adults and teenagers, particularly those involved with the Knights of Columbus, this journey of embracing may seem daunting. Yet it is precisely at this developmental stage where forming a real understanding of one's own identity is most crucial. Here, the teachings of the Theology of the Body offer not only clarity but also a roadmap for living out relationships with respect, integrity, and selfless love. As young members grow into their skills and capabilities, those choices made through the lens of this theology can lead to a life of purpose and fulfillment.

It helps to incorporate the support of community, for living out this theology is not meant to be a solitary endeavor. The communal aspect brings strength and solidarity. Within a faith community, such as that offered by the Knights of Columbus, members find shared values and the courage to embody these principles in a world that often values superficiality over substance. Here, training each member to view and treat their bodies as sacred is imbued with collective efforts that elevate personal struggles to noble missions.

Consider the moments spent in prayer and reflection. These are the spaces where embracing the theology deepens. Through practices such as meditation or participating in the sacraments, we open ourselves to the divine wisdom intended to inhabit all facets of our existence. These are not just moments of personal holiness, but also times when community comes alive, when personal reflections spill over into communal manifestations of faith.

What does this mean practically? It means finding Christ in everyday actions. Whether it be in a smile shared with a stranger, a listening ear offered to a friend, or the commitment to fairness and honesty in dealings, every act is an opportunity to honor this profound theological insight. We are invited to see everything—chores, obligations, interactions—as stages where God plays his finest symphony.

Moreover, embracing this theology does not mean denying life's challenges. On the contrary, it's about approaching struggles with a perspective that sees suffering not as abandonment but as an opportunity for redemptive love. In alignment with our faith, even suffering becomes a profound experience that prepares the heart for more compassionate encounters with others. There's power in understanding that our fragilities do not distance us from God but rather, bring us closer to His heart—a heart that we are called to reflect back into the world.

Perhaps most significantly, embracing the Theology of the Body nurtures discernment. In a culture of information overload and fast-paced living, taking the time to discern God's will is both liberating and grounding. Here, we learn to distinguish between the temporary allurements of the world and the enduring call to live authentically as God's children. This discernment becomes a beacon of grace, guiding our choices toward lives of fulfillment and holiness.

In conclusion, embracing the Theology of the Body is an invitation to see the world anew and live with intention. It calls for ongoing growth, taking a lifelong commitment bathed in grace. While each person's path in embodying these teachings may differ, the call remains the same: to live as true reflections of the divine, discovering God's voice in the everyday. This rich theology is not just knowledge to be possessed but love to be embodied, a transformation to be lived out amid the world and in the core of oneself.

Chapter 10: Overcoming Modern Challenges

Navigating the turbulent waters of today's world often feels like a daunting task for young Catholics seeking to live out the profound truths of the Theology of the Body. The pervasive influence of media and the growing secularism around us can cloud the vision of a life rooted in faith, making it increasingly vital for the Knights of Columbus to provide steadfast guidance. As modern challenges proliferate, it becomes crucial to harness the spirit of compassion and courage, empowering young adults and teenagers to see beyond the surface-level narratives they encounter daily. By fostering spaces of genuine dialogue and nurturing communities of faith, we can encourage a generation to hold fast to their beliefs. It is through the lens of love and responsibility that these challenges become not just obstacles to be overcome but opportunities for profound personal and spiritual growth. Embracing these trials, with the support of a community grounded in Gospel values, opens a path to maintaining integrity and a vibrant faith life even amidst the noise of modernity.

Media Influence on Youth

In our modern age, media permeates every aspect of daily life, shaping how we perceive the world and interact with each other. For young people, who are in the process of forming their identities and worldviews, the influence of media cannot be underestimated. As Roman Catholics and members of the Knights of Columbus, it's essential to understand and navigate these influences with wisdom and faith.

Let's consider the various forms of media that are omnipresent today: social media platforms, television shows, movies, music, and even advertisements. Each delivers messages that can either uplift or mislead. The challenge lies in discerning what aligns with Christian values and what contradicts them. This discernment is crucial in maintaining the dignity of the human person as made in the image of God, a concept deeply rooted in the Theology of the Body.

Firstly, social media is a double-edged sword. On one hand, it allows for connectivity and community building, breaking down geographical barriers and fostering global conversations. On the other, it often presents distorted images of success, beauty, and happiness. Young people might find themselves measuring their worth through likes, shares, and comments rather than intrinsic value gifted by God.

A proactive approach is needed. Encouraging youth to curate their feeds, follow faith-centered content, and engage with communities that promote healthy, Christ-centered values can make a significant difference. It's not about isolating oneself from the world, but engaging with it in a way that speaks truth and brings about positive change.

Television and movies, too, serve as powerful mediums shaping cultural perceptions. The narratives they provide can deeply influence beliefs and behaviors. While many shows and films promote themes of love and kindness, others might normalize actions that stray far from Christian virtues. Young viewers can learn to critically analyze what they are watching, asking questions such as, "Does this align with the teachings of Christ?" and "How does this reflect or obscure the concept of love and responsibility as taught by the Church?"

Critical thinking and open discussions within communities can empower young Catholics to become discerning consumers of media. Once they understand their faith more deeply, they can see through the lens of divine love and prevent toxic narratives from taking root in their hearts.

Music, another pervasive form of media, has the power to touch the soul profoundly. It stirs emotions and can inspire individuals towards greater things. Yet, some music promotes messages that glorify sin or devalue human dignity. By choosing music that uplifts the spirit and reflects the beauty of God's creation, youth can fill their hearts and minds with truth and goodness.

Engagement in creating media can also be transformative. Encouraging young Catholics to participate in creating art, music, films, or writing that reflects their values can spread hope and faith to others. By being creators, they directly influence culture and can use these platforms to witness and evangelize.

Advertisements, often overlooked, subtly influence buying habits, desires, and perceptions of necessity. Consumerism, driven by targeted advertising, can lead one away from a life of gratitude and simplicity. Understanding the nature of advertising helps young people make conscious choices about their consumption, steering them towards a life aligned with stewardhip and contentment.

Importantly, parents, educators, and the larger church community play vital roles in mediating the interaction between youth and media. Providing guidance, setting boundaries, and being role models are key to supporting youth in overcoming the challenges posed by media influence. Open dialogue and trust foster an environment where young people can ask questions and seek advice.

Ultimately, it's about transforming the challenge of media influence into an opportunity for deeper engagement with faith. The Theology of the Body offers a compelling foundation to view media: as tools for communicating God's love or, when misused, distortions that need careful navigation. Empowered with this understanding, youth can rise above the clamor of contradictory messages and live authentically in God's truth.

With the right perspective, media doesn't have to be a hindrance to spiritual growth. Instead, it can be a field of evangelization and witness. By embracing these challenges through the lens of faith, young Catholics can shine as beacons of hope, spreading the love and teachings of Christ in a world that desperately needs them.

Maintaining Faith in Secular World

We live in a world where the secular often takes center stage in our daily lives. It seems like everywhere we turn, there are new challenges to our faith and beliefs. But despite these challenges, maintaining our faith is not just essential; it's fundamental to how we live as Roman Catholics. This faith is not just a private affair but one that inevitably shapes how we see the world and respond to its challenges. To navigate this secular landscape effectively, young Catholics must engage with society without losing the essence of their beliefs.

In a culture where media and societal norms often promote a way of life that contradicts our teachings, it's easy to feel isolated or even tempted to compromise. The key to resilience lies in internalizing our faith so deeply that it becomes an inseparable part of our identity. Our faith is more than rituals or doctrines; it's a living relationship with Christ. By constantly nurturing this relationship through prayer, Scripture, and the sacraments, we can find the strength to remain steadfast.

Catholics are called to be in the world, but not of it. This means engaging with the contemporary world, understanding its gifts and its pitfalls, yet remaining anchored in our faith. The challenge is to embrace what is good and true while resisting elements that pull us away from God. Embracing our identity as children of God means living out our faith visibly and courageously, unafraid to be different when the need arises.

One practical approach to maintaining faith is building a solid community. The Church has always emphasized the importance of community, for there is strength in numbers. Whether it's through parish activities, Knights of Columbus gatherings, or young adult groups, being a part of a community provides support and encouragement. In these circles, we find others who share our values and can offer guidance and friendship.

Moreover, individuals must focus on personal spiritual development. A daily habit of prayer and meditation can center us, keeping us in tune with God's will. The sacraments, especially Eucharist and Reconciliation, are pillars that sustain us, providing grace for the journey. Regular participation aligns our daily struggles with God's larger plan, reminding us that we are not alone, and He is with us.

"Faith without works is dead." This biblical reminder is a call to action. In a secular world, our actions often speak louder than words. Living authentically as people of faith means acting with love and integrity, even when it's difficult or unpopular. Our lives should be a testimony to the transformative power of faith, inspiring others not through what we say, but through how we live.

The education provided through the Theology of the Body curriculum has a vital role here. By understanding the inherent dignity that comes with being created in God's image, young adults can develop a profound respect for themselves and others. This respect then fuels a desire to make choices that uphold this dignity in every aspect of their lives—from relationships to career choices.

Engagement with modern media platforms also requires a discernment of what is beneficial and what is harmful. The digital age provides incredible opportunities for evangelization and learning, yet it's also rife with distractions and distortions of truth. By approaching these platforms with prudence and a critical eye, grounded in solid catechesis, we can discern what aligns with our beliefs and what detracts from them.

The teachings of our faith are not a series of restrictions but are pathways to true freedom and joy. By embracing them fully, young Catholics can find a purpose and meaning that transcends the shallow promises of a secular lifestyle. This transformation doesn't happen overnight. It's a journey of highs and lows, a testament of faith in action. By leaning on the examples of saints and drawing strength from the community, Catholics can persevere.

In facing a world that often values the material over the spiritual, Catholics are tasked with contributing a different narrative—one that showcases the peace and fulfillment found in Christ. As the Knights of Columbus continue their mission, they carry the banner of faith proudly. Their work with young adults will be crucial in shaping a generation that doesn't shy away from the challenges of the modern world but meets them with faith and courage.

Ultimately, maintaining faith in a secular world is about choice. It's a daily commitment to live in a way that reflects God's love and truth. It's about choosing to see the sacred in the ordinary and finding God's presence in the midst of what seems overwhelmingly secular. It's about recognizing that every small step in faith contributes to a larger journey of transformation.

Let us take comfort and find inspiration in the words of Christ who assured us, "In the world you will have tribulation. But take heart; I have overcome the world." Buoyed by this promise, young Catholics can go forth with confidence, rooted in a faith that illuminates even the most ordinary of moments with extraordinary grace.

Chapter 11: Science and the Body

In a world where science and faith are often seen as opposing forces, understanding the harmony between them is crucial, especially when it comes to our own bodies. As Roman Catholics, we know that our bodies are not just biological entities but are temples of the Holy Spirit, deserving of reverence and care. The intersection of science and faith invites us to explore human biology through the lens of divine creation. In recognizing the complexities of our physiological makeup, we marvel not only at genetic codes and cellular processes but also at God's intricate design and intentions for us. Science offers insights into how our bodies function, while faith imbues these insights with purpose and meaning, guiding us to live our lives in truth and love. The thoughtful integration of these perspectives helps us to foster a holistic appreciation of our physical selves, encouraging a respect that mirrors the infinite worth bestowed upon us by our Creator. When we approach science with faith, we don't just uncover the mechanics of life; we discover a profound affinity with the divine plan, one that calls us to act as stewards of our health and well-being.

Human Biology through Faith's Lens

Human biology, when viewed through the lens of faith, reveals profound truths about our existence and purpose. The physical structures that constitute our bodies are not merely organic mechanisms operating in a vacuum; they are expressions of divine artistry and wisdom. Pope Saint John Paul II, through his teachings on the Theology of the Body, invited us to explore the body's dignity and its role in manifesting God's love. Our bodies are the temple of the Holy Spirit, intricately woven to serve as a testament of divine creation. In this understanding, faith and science converge, complementing rather than contradicting each other.

At the heart of this exploration is the recognition that human beings are made in the image and likeness of God. This is not a mere spiritual abstraction but manifests in the very fibers of our human composition. Our flesh and blood, our very biology, bear the mark of divine creativity. To view our biological processes as anything less than sacred would be to miss the magnificence of God's design. In this way, science, far from diminishing our spiritual significance, actually enhances our appreciation for it.

Reflecting on human development, for instance, we witness a miraculous transformation from a single cell to a complex organism capable of thought, emotion, and action. The intricate dance of cells, the development of organs, and the syncing of bodily systems demonstrate an intelligent design that exceeds human understanding. From conception to the natural end, every stage of life reveals divine intention and purpose. Embracing our biology through faith thus allows us to see not just the physical, but the metaphysical dimensions of our humanity.

Faith tells us that our legitimate interest in understanding the body should inspire gratitude toward the Creator, not hubris. As we uncover the mysteries of the human genome or the workings of the brain, we approach a deeper reverence for the complexity and wonder of human life. The Knights of Columbus, in shepherding this vision, have a unique role. They are called not just to protect life but to elucidate its inherent sanctity. Educating young people in this truth helps to form a generation that values life in its totality, recognizing each person as a sacred gift.

In this light, science becomes a testament to the wonder of God's creation, offering evidence of our unique place within it. Despite living in a world driven by empirical validation, there's a profound acknowledgment that our understanding remains incomplete without integrating faith. Faith illuminates that which science observes, granting principled direction and deeper meaning. As such, a faithful perspective on human biology doesn't shun scientific inquiry but rather invites a collaboration that edifies both domains.

Consider the dynamism of the human heart—a biological marvel incessantly pulsing life throughout the body. The heart, beyond its physical prowess, is often seen as the seat of emotion and will within our spiritual traditions. This interplay between physical and metaphysical aspects reminds us that our existence can't be divorced from the purposeful love with which God created us. Such a perspective encourages young Catholics to honor their bodies and integrate their faith with an understanding of science.

Our sensual experiences, too, are enriched through a faith perspective. God crafted our senses not just for survival, but to experience and engage with His creation fully. Seeing, hearing, touching, tasting, and smelling draw us into a relational experience with the world, inviting us to respond with gratitude and reverence. When we open our hearts to this understanding, even mundane biological processes become opportunities for recognizing God's handiwork.

Moreover, human vulnerability and suffering, elements that biology doesn't skirt, find fuller context here. Faith teaches that suffering is not devoid of purpose but can lead to profound personal transformation and spiritual growth. Our biological frailties—those moments when science meets its limits—invite us into a deeper trust in God's providential care. It's a call to see beyond the limitations of the flesh to the potential of our spirit empowered by grace.

As educators and mentors, understanding human biology through faith offers a way to teach the dignity of the human person. The Knights of Columbus are thereby entrusted with nurturing a curriculum that promotes respect for the body as something more than a physical vessel but as a precious gift from God. Teaching this to teenagers and young adults equips them with the moral compass to navigate contemporary challenges such as bioethical questions, consumerism of body image, and technological influence on human life.

Looking at the intersection of faith and human biology offers a holistic approach to life that seeks the truth, goodness, and beauty inherent in God's creation. It reminds us that each individual, fearfully and wonderfully made, holds infinite value and should be treated with the utmost respect and love. Thus, integrating a faith perspective in understanding human biology isn't just an academic exercise—it's foundational to living a life that reflects the profound mystery of God's love realized in our human form.

Intersection of Faith and Science

The relationship between faith and science has been a topic of contemplation and exploration for centuries, yet it remains as relevant today as ever, especially when we consider its implications on our understanding of the human body. Faith and science, far from being contradictory, often intersect in profound ways, contributing to a richer and more holistic understanding of what it means to be human. The Catholic perspective uniquely bridges these domains, affirming that scientific discoveries can illuminate the wonders of God's creation while faith provides a moral compass.

To begin, let's consider the body itself—a masterpiece of divine craftsmanship. Science provides us with an intricate glimpse of the body's complexities, from the cellular level to entire systems working harmoniously to maintain life. This complexity invites awe and deepens respect for the Creator. While science equips us with the tools to explore these wonders, faith invites us to ponder their ultimate purpose and meaning. Here lies the intersection: scientific exploration becomes an act of worship when seen through the lens of faith.

Faith and science both seek truth, albeit through different means. Science pursues empirical evidence, building on observable and testable phenomena. Faith seeks truth beyond the material, probing the spiritual and moral dimensions of life. Yet, both disciplines nourish an understanding of human dignity and the sanctity of life. Science, for instance, underscores the biological uniqueness of each individual, reinforcing the theological insight that every person is created in the image of God and imbued with inherent worth.

One can observe this harmony in the medical field. Catholic healthcare systems embody this synthesis, emphasizing not just physical healing but also spiritual care. Professionals in these settings are often motivated by their faith to treat each patient with dignity, recognizing the sacredness of every life. Advances in medicine, such as genetic research, have opened up new avenues for healing and prevention, consistently guided by ethical considerations rooted in Catholic teaching. This moral framework guards against practices that undermine human dignity, such as cloning or unchecked genetic manipulation.

A compelling aspect of this intersection is how scientific understanding can inform ethical decisions in healthcare and technology. For instance, concepts like informed consent and patient autonomy are enriched by a faith-informed perspective that highlights the person's inviolable dignity. Faith-filled scientists and healthcare practitioners are called to uphold these principles as they navigate complex situations, ensuring that technological advancements serve the common good.

Additionally, faith challenges science to remain humble in its assertions. While scientific progress has achieved remarkable feats, it doesn't possess all the answers to life's deepest questions. Faith acknowledges mystery, accepting that not every truth can be quantified or explained. This humility encourages scientists to recognize the limits of their discipline and remain open to spiritual and philosophical insights.

Furthermore, the dialogue between faith and science promotes environmental stewardship. As science reveals the delicate balance of ecosystems and the impact of human actions, faith reminds us of our responsibility to care for creation as stewards entrusted by God. By collaborating, science and faith inspire sustainable practices that respect the interconnectedness of all life and reverence for the earth.

In educational settings, this intersection can inspire young minds to appreciate both the rigor of scientific inquiry and the richness of faith tradition. Encouraging teenagers and young adults to engage with both disciplines fosters critical thinking and moral development. It invites them to see scientific pursuits not as contrary to their beliefs but as complementary ways to engage with their world and their Creator.

Ultimately, contemplating the intersection of faith and science leads us to a deeper understanding of our own bodies as temples of the Holy Spirit. As we unlock scientific mysteries, we are invited to appreciate more fully the gift of life and to embrace a profound sense of gratitude and responsibility for how we live. By embracing both rational inquiry and spiritual wisdom, we can better articulate a vision of human flourishing that honors both God and His creation.

Chapter 12: Prayer and Meditation

In the bustling world young adults and teenagers navigate, carving out moments for prayer and meditation becomes crucial to nurturing their spiritual growth. This chapter explores the profound simplicity of connecting with God through personal reflection and quiet devotion, a practice deeply embedded in our Catholic tradition. Prayer isn't just about reciting words; it's a heartfelt dialogue with the Divine, inviting His presence into the intricacies of daily life. Meditation allows us to linger in His presence, opening our hearts to listen intently and discern His guidance amidst the chaos. As Knights of Columbus, fostering a prayerful life offers a compass for the younger generation, guiding them towards a life of virtue and purpose. Through guided prayers and meditations, we learn to center our lives on Christ and draw strength from the wells of grace He offers. This commitment transforms not just individuals but communities, weaving a fabric of faith that upholds and sustains us all.

Developing a Prayerful Life

In our diverse and fast-paced world, developing a prayerful life can feel like an uphill battle. It's easy to get caught up in the whirlwind of daily responsibilities and distractions, which might make setting aside time for prayer seem like an impossible task. Yet, when we pause and reflect, prayer becomes not just a duty, but an essential lifeline—a connection to the divine that sustains us through all seasons of life. Building a prayerful existence is about integrating moments of silence and reflection into our everyday routine, turning it into an enriching habit rather than a checkbox to tick.

For young adults and teenagers, prayer offers a unique opportunity to anchor their faith during a crucial phase of their lives. As they navigate the complexities of growing up, prayer can provide clarity and purpose. Embracing a prayerful life as young Knights of Columbus means growing in spiritual maturity, aligning one's life with values that transcend fleeting societal trends. It's about standing firm in your beliefs, strengthened by a relationship with God that manifests through regular prayer.

So, how does one cultivate this sacred practice? The first step is to acknowledge and accept the profound need for prayer, not as a chore, but as a response to God's invitation for communion. Just like any good relationship, prayer requires dedication and time. Yet, it's essential to approach it with an open heart and mind, ready to listen and speak to God, even amidst life's chaos.

Creating a space of prayer can significantly enhance one's ability to focus on the divine. This doesn't mean having a physical space alone, though a quiet corner with minimal distractions can be beneficial. It also suggests creating mental and emotional room to welcome God's presence. Whether it's during an early morning walk, a quiet evening retreat, or even while commuting, identifying and nurturing these prayerful moments is key.

Prayer, in its truest sense, is deeply personal—but it also has a communal aspect that's crucial within the context of the Knights of Columbus. Group prayer and meditation sessions can inspire young Catholics to engage actively in their faith community. By sharing in each other's spiritual journeys, individuals can draw strength from collective faith experiences. This not only reinforces personal prayer habits but also strengthens community bonds, united in purpose and faith.

As young people flesh out their own prayerful lives, the types of prayers they engage with can vary widely. Some might find solace in traditional prayers—the rosary or the liturgy of the hours—while others may be drawn to more spontaneous forms of conversation with God. What's important is finding the right balance that resonates with personal spirituality and circumstances.

Moreover, prayer isn't just about speaking; it's also about listening. Meditation, as part of a prayerful life, involves more than just quiet moments; it's about silencing the internal noise to truly hear God's voice. For teenagers, accustomed to perpetual stimulus from digital devices and media, learning to be still and listen can significantly deepen their relationship with the divine.

Incorporating prayer in daily life shouldn't feel burdensome. If anything, it should be a refreshing refuge—a source of strength and renewal. Setting regular times for prayer can turn it into a routine that naturally integrates into one's lifestyle. This might be as simple as beginning the day with a few moments of gratitude or ending it with a reflection on blessings received.

The Knights of Columbus can play a pivotal role by offering resources and guidance to help young adults and teenagers maintain their prayerful practices. Workshops on prayer techniques, meditation sessions, and access to spiritual mentors can greatly benefit those striving to deepen their connections with God.

A lifelong journey of prayer is filled with ebb and flow. There will be times when the spiritual connection feels strong, and other times when it seems elusive. This is natural and part of the growth process. Perseverance, even during spiritually desolate times, can lead to profound spiritual maturity and strength. It's these moments that often refine and strengthen one's faith.

In conclusion, developing a prayerful life is about cultivating an intimate dialogue with God amidst life's clamor. It requires patience, an open heart, and a sincere desire to walk closely with the Almighty. The journey is immensely personal yet enriched immensely by communal support and shared experiences. For the young Knights of Columbus, a prayerful life is not just an aspiration but a pathway to living a full, faith-filled existence aligned with the tenets of Theology of the Body. Through discipline, faith, and community engagement, they can achieve a transformative relationship with God that guides them through life's trials and triumphs.

Guided Prayers and Meditations

As we delve into the realm of guided prayers and meditations, we journey towards building a deeper connection with God, one that fosters both spiritual growth and personal reflection. These practices anchor us, offering a steady presence in an often tumultuous world. For Roman Catholics, particularly the Knights of Columbus and young adults seeking to develop a Theology of the Body curriculum, guided prayers serve as spiritual compasses, nurturing a pathway to understanding one's purpose and vocation.

The act of prayer is less about perfectly crafted words and more about intentional communion with the Divine. When practicing guided prayers, the humility of acknowledging our need for God stands paramount, opening our hearts to spiritual nourishment. Such intentional prayers can provide structure, allowing us to meditate on the nuances of the Theology of the Body, particularly as it pertains to understanding our own dignity and the sacredness of our bodies.

Guided meditations, in a similar vein, serve as a conduit for peace and clarity. Through meditative practices, we invite God into the silence of our minds and hearts, creating a space to listen and receive guidance. Consider focusing on a specific passage from the Bible or a piece of sacred imagery. Open your heart to reflect on what Christ's presence in your life might mean in the context of your relationships, your vocation, and your journey of faith.

Integrating guided meditations into your daily routine doesn't have to be a grand affair. Start small, perhaps with a few minutes each morning or evening dedicated to sitting in silence, breathing deeply, and setting your intentions. As you progress, you may find these moments expanding, becoming central, and vital to your daily life. This consistent practice cultivates resilience against modern challenges, serving as a steadfast reminder of our worth and the divine love that envelops us.

Incorporating prayer and meditation with others can also enhance these practices. Consider gathering with a group of fellow Knights or young adults for a shared session. Such moments of communal prayer not only strengthen personal faith but also build a support network, a community bound by shared experiences and aspirations. Engage in discussions afterward, sharing insights or revelations that arose during your meditations. It's in these shared narratives that we often find fresh perspectives and deepen our understanding of the Theology of the Body.

For teenagers and young adults, prayer and meditation also offer a shelter amidst the whirlwind of peer pressure and modern-day distractions. By establishing a strong foundation of these practices, young Catholics empower themselves to make choices that align with their values and beliefs, resisting temptations that diverge from their spiritual path. This empowerment isn't just about avoiding what's wrong; it's about actively pursuing what's right, grounded in the understanding of our bodies as temples of the Holy Spirit.

A simple yet profound guided meditation can involve focusing on the breath while repeating a phrase or prayer. For instance, use the Jesus Prayer – "Lord Jesus Christ, have mercy on me" – aligning the words to your inhalation and exhalation. This rhythmic repetition allows the prayer to settle deeply within your heart, offering a sense of calm and an assurance of God's abiding presence.

Sometimes, incorporating physical movement into prayer, like in the practice of the Rosary or walking meditations, can enhance the experience. Walking with intentionality through nature while contemplating God's creation infuses our prayer life with the vibrancy of the world around us, reminding us of our connection to every living thing. Such practices enrich our understanding of the Theology of the Body by illustrating the interconnectedness of all creation.

An essential tool in guided meditations is Lectio Divina, an ancient practice of scriptural reading, meditation, and prayer intended to promote communion with God. By engaging with sacred texts through reading, meditation, prayer, and contemplation, we allow the Word to transform us, aligning our daily actions with the profound truths found in Scripture. This disciplined approach encourages a personal dialogue with God, prompting self-reflection and spiritual awakening.

Furthermore, the use of sacred art in meditation provides a visual dimension that can stir the soul. Viewing a painting depicting the Annunciation or the Last Supper, and meditating on its significance, can transport us to new spiritual heights. These visual storytellers have a unique way of resonating within our hearts, deepening our appreciation for the divine story of salvation and our place within it.

By fostering a habit of guided prayers and meditations, we engage in an ongoing conversion, continually redirecting our hearts to God and aligning our lives with His divine will. This sacred practice not only aids personal spiritual development but also equips us to bear witness to our faith in the world, reinforcing the Knights of Columbus' mission of charity, unity, and fraternity.

Ultimately, these prayerful practices become powerful tools for discernment, helping us navigate life's myriad choices, and fulfilling our vocation to love as embodied in the Theology of the Body. Whether in the stillness of solitary prayer or the vibrant interplay of group meditations, such devotions remind us of our intrinsic value and our calling to embody the love of Christ in our lives.

May our journey through guided prayers and meditations draw us ever closer to our Creator, enriching our faith, and illuminating the beauty of living according to the tenets of the Theology of the Body. Let this practice be a foundation upon which we build not only personal holiness but also a vibrant, faith-filled community that reflects the very essence of God's love and wisdom.

Chapter 13: Forgiveness and Healing

In the journey of faith, forgiveness emerges as an unparalleled expression of divine love, offering a path to both personal and communal healing. At its core, forgiveness is an active choice born out of love; it requires vulnerability yet leads to a restoration of grace that reflects the ultimate sacrifice of Christ. When we forgive, we participate in God's mercy, creating space for reconciliation and peace that echoes in eternity. Healing, then, is not simply the absence of hurt, but the profound transformation of our hearts towards compassion and empathy. It's in the willingness to forgive that we dismantle barriers and engage in authentic encounters, bringing to life the promise of Christ that love triumphs over all. As Knights and young believers, embracing this sacred practice equips us to heal relationships and manifest the theology of the body in a world thirsting for genuine connection. Through the lens of forgiveness, we witness Christ's presence anew, urging us to courageously weave our individual stories into the greater opus of God's redeeming plan.

Power of Forgiveness

When we consider the power of forgiveness, we're diving into one of the most transformative aspects of human experience. Within the Christian faith, forgiveness is more than a moral or emotional concept; it's a profound spiritual force imbued with the ability to heal, restore, and renew. To understand its magnitude is to grasp a part of the divine mystery of love, which calls each of us to a higher standard of living and interacting with others.

Forgiveness offers a path to freedom. It liberates us from the chains of resentment and bitterness, freeing both the one who forgives and the one who is forgiven. This liberation doesn't mean that we forget the wrongs done to us, but that we choose not to be prisoners of hurt and anger. It's a courageous decision to live in peace and grace, reflecting the ultimate act of love Jesus demonstrated on the cross when He forgave those who crucified Him.

In our modern world, where hurt and divisiveness often dominate, forgiveness appears almost countercultural. Yet, for those aspiring to live a life inspired by the Theology of the Body, committing to forgiveness is not optional; it's essential. Forgiveness is a testament to faith in action, intertwining the earthly with the divine and bringing heaven closer to our daily lives.

We encounter this need for forgiveness in our everyday relationships—be it with family, friends, or even strangers. In these interactions, misunderstandings and disagreements are inevitable. But how we handle them can make all the difference. Embracing forgiveness allows us to see beyond the immediate pain and recognize the intrinsic worth of the other person, created in the image of God, just as we are.

At times, the most challenging person to forgive is oneself. Self-forgiveness requires an acceptance of our flaws and a trust in God's infinite mercy. It's a process of understanding that our worth is not diminished by our mistakes. By forgiving ourselves, we open the door to spiritual growth, enabling us to extend genuine forgiveness to others. This mutual healing enriches our vocations, strengthens our communities, and furthers the Knights of Columbus' mission to foster unity and charity.

The Saints provide inspiring examples of the power of forgiveness. St. Maria Goretti, who forgave her attacker on her deathbed, and Maximilian Kolbe, whose martyrdom was an ultimate act of love and forgiveness, both reveal the transformative potential that forgiveness holds. These examples illuminate the path for us, teaching that true strength lies in mercy and compassion.

Incorporating forgiveness into our daily lives, especially as young adults and teenagers, is critical for cultivating authentic relationships and building a vibrant community. It's a practice that starts small—a conversation, an apology, a hug—yet holds the promise of profound impact. As members of the Knights of Columbus and followers of Christ, this principle can guide us in bringing about reconciliation and healing in a world deeply in need of both.

Forgiveness is not a solitary journey. It's a communal experience that mirrors the Eucharist, where we seek unity and reconciliation with God and with each other. This communal aspect reinforces the importance of support and encouragement from our faith communities as we strive to embody forgiveness in all aspects of life.

The Power of Forgiveness, then, lies not only in its capacity to mend and restore but also in its ability to inspire and transform. As we embrace this powerful gift, we continue building a life that reflects the divine love and mercy God has shown us. By doing so, we weave a tapestry of hope and healing, resounding with the grace of God's unending love.

Steps to Emotional Healing

Emotionally healing from past wounds is a journey that demands courage and patience. Forgiveness and healing are intertwined in a journey that, though challenging, leads to peace and wholeness. Healing starts with acknowledging the pain. This might seem obvious, but in a world that often encourages us to "move on," acknowledging our pain is a crucial and brave step. It's about facing wounds that, like any physical injury, need proper care and attention. Instead of pushing feelings aside, we invite them into the light, giving them space in our hearts.

In this process, prayer is an essential companion. It anchors us, nurturing our relationship with God, who understands the depth of our hurt. Through prayer, we invite God into our journey, asking Him to provide strength and guidance. It's both a shelter in moments of raw vulnerability and a way to gain insight and solace. During prayer, we can express our emotions freely, knowing God listens with compassion and understanding.

After acknowledgment, embracing the act of forgiveness becomes the next step in healing. Forgiveness is more than a mere dismissal of wrongs; it's an act of release. This release does not absolve others of accountability but frees us from an emotional burden. We forgive, not for others, but for ourselves, to clear the path of grievances that obstruct our peace. It's a spiritual decision to say "I will not let this hold me back."

Reflecting on the lives of saints can offer comfort and guidance. Saints like Maximilian Kolbe and Therese of Lisieux faced hardships yet responded with love and compassion. Drawing inspiration from their lives empowers us to approach forgiveness with a mindset of love rather than retaliation. Their lives remind us of the transformative power of forgiving with grace.

Sharing our experiences with others can illuminate our path to healing. Confiding in trusted friends, spiritual advisors, or therapists fosters a sense of community and supports healing. Engaging with those who listen actively and empathetically helps us process our emotions. This interaction validates our experiences and diminishes feelings of isolation.

Building a practice of mindfulness is valuable for emotional healing. By being present, we can examine our emotions without judgment, understanding that feelings are temporary yet insightful. Practicing mindfulness allows us to acknowledge difficult emotions as they arise and let them pass without clinging on to them. This practice nurtures patience and helps us develop resilience over time.

It is important to replace negative emotions with positive actions. Acts of kindness, service, and love can fill the void left by pain. Engaging in loving actions for others brightens our spirit and helps reconnect us to the world around us. This is a testament to finding purpose and fulfillment beyond our pain. It embodies a vital shift from consuming bitterness to creating joy.

Healing also involves acknowledging areas in life where we need change. It's a time to evaluate relationships, practices, and habits that may hinder our emotional flourishing. By recognizing these areas, we pave the way for personal growth and create a supportive environment for ongoing healing. Sometimes, limiting contact with negative influences or changing certain life aspects is necessary for your well-being.

Ultimately, healing is ongoing and doesn't follow a linear path. It requires taking time and being gentle with oneself, acknowledging setbacks without letting them define our journey. Each person's path to emotional healing is unique and should be respected. Walking this path alongside our faith ensures that no matter the pace, we are progressing towards a greater wholeness and understanding.

Though challenging, working through emotional healing with determination allows us to reclaim parts of ourselves that we may have lost along the way. The journey becomes not just a means to cope, but an opportunity for transformation, preparing us to embrace our lives with renewed vigor and faith. Summit the mountain of forgiveness and healing by taking that first step today and be assured that every step forward, no matter how small, is a victory.

Chapter 14: Peer Influence and Personal Growth

As we journey through life, the presence and influence of peers become a powerful force molding our character and faith. This chapter delves into how young Catholics can navigate peer pressure while staying rooted in their values and growing in their relationship with God. Within the supportive embrace of the Knights of Columbus and the broader Catholic community, young people find themselves uniquely positioned to cultivate resilience and authenticity. It is here that the seeds of personal growth are sown, encouraged by a faith that nurtures rather than confines. Through shared experiences and intentional fellowship, individuals are called to reflect Christ's love, allowing them to thrive despite societal pressures. This interplay between personal decisions and communal support fosters a vibrant faith life, inspiring each person to become a beacon of light and hope to those around them.

Navigating Peer Pressure

Peer pressure is a powerful force that can shape our decisions, sometimes subtly and other times, with overwhelming intensity. It's a reality that teenagers and young adults face as they strive to live out their faith in a world full of diverse influences. Recognizing the impact of peer pressure is the first step towards navigating it successfully. The teachings of the Theology of the Body provide a strong foundation, enabling young Catholics to draw on their faith as a guiding compass in these crucial moments.

Peer pressure can manifest in many ways—from the pressure to conform to certain behaviors or attitudes, to the influence of cultural trends that may not align with Christian values. It challenges us to stand firm in our beliefs while also maintaining relationships. The Knights of Columbus have long understood this struggle, providing support and education to help young believers remain steadfast in their faith journey. It's essential to remember that while peer pressure can feel isolating, nobody has to face these challenges alone.

In the Scriptures, we find countless examples of individuals who faced peer pressure and chose to follow God's path instead. Whether it's the courage of Daniel in the lion's den or Mary's faithful fiat, these stories inspire and remind us that staying true to our values can lead to profound growth and fulfillment. Embracing such biblical examples enriches our understanding of how to live authentically, without compromising our beliefs under societal pressures.

To counteract the negative effects of peer pressure, young Catholics are encouraged to build a support network of like-minded individuals who share similar goals and values. Community plays a crucial role, offering encouragement and accountability. The Knights of Columbus foster such communities, emphasizing the importance of fellowship in combating negative influences. Engaging in community prayer, discussions, and activities helps solidify one's identity rooted in Christ.

Developing a clear sense of identity—knowing who you are and what you stand for—is vital. Young Catholics can draw on their identity as children of God, using this as their anchor in turbulent times. The Theology of the Body teaches us that our dignity is inherent and not determined by others' opinions or expectations. This theological understanding empowers individuals to resist the temptation to compromise their principles for the sake of acceptance or popularity.

Moreover, building resilience against peer pressure involves cultivating internal virtues such as courage, wisdom, and self-control. These virtues fortify our ability to discern and make choices that align with our faith. Both St. Maximilian Kolbe and St. Thérèse of Lisieux exemplified these virtues in their lives. By studying their examples, young people can be inspired to embrace their challenges with grace and fortitude.

Choosing friends wisely is another practical approach to navigating peer pressure. Surrounding oneself with friends who respect and support one's faith journey creates a positive environment that diminishes the pull of negative peer influences. Relationships based on mutual respect and shared values are more likely to encourage rather than compromise one's principles.

Open communication with trusted mentors, such as parents, priests, or youth leaders, provides additional support. Discussing the pressures faced in daily life allows for new perspectives and guidance rooted in Catholic teachings. Sometimes, having an outside view can illuminate pathways through difficult experiences, shedding light on how best to apply the principles of the Theology of the Body to personal challenges.

Technology and social media, too, play significant roles in peer influence, often amplifying both positive and negative pressures. Understanding the impact of these platforms and learning to use them responsibly is key. Practicing discernment when engaging online can help maintain one's integrity. It's about being authentic to one's true self and the values hold dear, even when every 'like' and comment might suggest otherwise.

Of course, prayer and meditation form the cornerstone of resisting pressure, offering peace and clarity amid chaos. Engaging in regular prayer not only strengthens one's relationship with God but also provides a sanctuary from external pressures. It's a reminder of the bigger picture—our call to live in fullness with Christ. Such spiritual practices develop an inner strength that's far deeper than any external pull might seem to possess.

Ultimately, navigating peer pressure through the lens of the Theology of the Body isn't just about resistance; it's about transformation. It's about allowing every challenge to deepen our faith, refine our character, and draw us closer to God. In facing peer pressure with courage and faith, teenagers and young adults not only protect their spiritual integrity but also become beacons of hope and examples for others.

Through the collective wisdom of saints and the teachings of the Church, young Catholics can feel empowered against any pressure that seeks to lead them astray. Embracing one's identity in Christ and living out the Theology of the Body equips young believers to walk confidently in faith, no matter what pressures the world might bring. As the Knights of Columbus continue to nurture such growth, they ensure a future where youth are not just surviving but thriving in their spiritual journeys.

Growing in Faith and Character

In the tumultuous journey from adolescence to adulthood, the nurturing of faith and character is indispensable. These formative years are when values and beliefs are molded, sometimes in the face of peer pressure and societal expectations. This section aims to shine a light on how young Roman Catholics, especially those involved with the Knights of Columbus, can embrace the growth of their faith and character amid the various influences they encounter.

First and foremost, understanding that personal growth is a divine calling can be a game-changer. It's not just about acquiring virtues or strengthening one's resolve but about realizing that this journey is intimately tied to one's purpose in God's creation. As teenagers and young adults chart their paths, the teachings of the Church can serve as a compass, guiding them through the complexities of modern life.

This growth in faith and character requires intentionality. It's essential to seek out environments and relationships that foster spiritual and moral development. Being part of the Knights of Columbus offers a unique community where like-minded individuals can support one another. Through fellowship, one can be held accountable and inspired by others who strive to lead lives that reflect the principles of Christ.

Beyond community support, personal prayer and reflection are vital. It's in these moments of solitude and communion with God that individuals can discern His will and gain the strength needed to persevere. Encouraging regular prayer or meditative practices, even if it's as simple as a few minutes each day, can cultivate a deep-rooted faith that withstands external pressures.

Exposure to sacred texts and writings from Church tradition also contributes to this spiritual growth. The profound teachings within the Gospel and the Saints' writings provide timeless wisdom and practical guidance. Practical knowledge acquired through these readings can serve as the foundation upon which strong, virtuous character is built.

As young Catholics strive to grow in faith and character, they often face challenges from peers that might test their values. It's not unusual to encounter varying worldviews and moral approaches that could sway one away from their spiritual path. The key is to remain steadfast in one's beliefs, using them as an anchor in a sea of conflicting messages and pressures.

Developing a character that reflects one's faith involves practicing virtues such as patience, kindness, and humility. These virtues act as moral fortifications, framing one's interactions and decisions. However, embodying these qualities is easier said than done, and thus, it is through persistent effort and prayer that they become ingrained in everyday life.

Peer influence can be a double-edged sword. While it might sometimes appear to deter one's faith journey, it can also inspire and uplift. By surrounding oneself with peers who exhibit strong principles and a steadfast commitment to their faith, young adults and teenagers can find role models whose actions speak louder than words. Witnessing someone living authentically and in alignment with their Catholic faith can act as a catalyst for personal growth.

Participating in community service and outreach activities also plays a crucial role. Engaging in such work allows young people to step outside themselves, to practice compassion, and to bear witness to Christ's love in action. These experiences not only build character but can also ignite a deeper passion for one's faith as they see firsthand the impact of living according to Gospel values.

Understanding that growing in faith and character is an ongoing process helps in appreciating the journey itself. It's about progress, not perfection. Every challenge faced, every victory won in the day-to-day walk with Christ contributes to an ever-deepening faith and stronger character.

Finally, it's crucial to have mentors or spiritual advisers who can guide and provide counsel. Someone older and wiser in faith can offer perspectives and insights that only come with experience. These guiding lights in one's life can reassure during moments of doubt and share invaluable lessons learned on their own journeys.

In conclusion, growing in faith and character is a sacred commitment that young Catholics must willingly embark upon. The influence of peers, the teachings of the Church, and personal devotion are all interwoven in this journey. As young members of the Knights of Columbus, standing firm in their beliefs and continuously striving to embody Christ's teachings, they set the stage for a life that not only honors God but also serves as a beacon of hope and strength to others. Consistent growth and learning can transform these years into a significant and spiritually enriching adventure.

Chapter 15: Developing Virtues

In our ongoing journey to live out the rich teachings of the Theology of the Body, developing virtues serves as the bedrock for a life rooted in faith and character. Virtues, those habitual and firm dispositions to do good, transform us from within and shine as beacons of grace leading us along the path of holiness. The Knights of Columbus, with their steadfast commitment to forming young minds, provide a powerful example of how virtues like courage, temperance, justice, and prudence can illuminate the heart and mind, directing them towards the divine purpose within. Even in a world full of noise and distraction, teenagers and young adults are invited to discover and nurture these virtues through focused exercises and lived experiences, helping them to not just understand, but truly embody their identity as bearers of God's image. This transformative process requires effort and intention, yet the reward is a deeper sense of fulfillment and readiness to face life's challenges with faith and determination.

Identifying Key Virtues

In our journey through life, recognizing and nurturing key virtues stand as a cornerstone in shaping our character and aligning with the teachings of Theology of the Body. True to the mission of forming young minds, identifying these virtues provides a compass guiding us toward a life enriched with purpose, dignity, and love. The task is not merely academic; it is a transformative process that inspires concrete actions and personal growth.

Virtues, in their purest form, can be viewed as habits or dispositions that lead us to act in ways that reflect our highest ideals. Within the fabric of Christian teaching, cardinal virtues such as prudence, justice, fortitude, and temperance serve as fundamental building blocks for ethical living. These virtues, while deeply rooted in philosophical thought, find profound expression in the Gospel and the teachings of the Church. They call us to nurture our choices with wisdom and courage, to love generously, and to act with integrity in all our interactions.

Identifying key virtues is not a one-size-fits-all endeavor; it is a deeply personal quest that requires introspection and openness to divine guidance. As members of the Knights of Columbus, young adults are invited to journey inwardly, exploring how virtues can be lived out daily. This involves engaging with both the chivalric spirit and the call to holiness, embodying virtues that are not only essential but also actively lived by our predecessors in faith.

Prudence, often called the "charioteer of all virtues," is fundamental in making sound decisions. As we navigate the complexities of modern life, prudence equips us with discernment, enabling us to accurately judge our actions and their potential impacts. In a world teeming with varied values and conflicting ideals, prudence sharpens our vision, helping us to remain steadfast in our faith and true to our moral compass.

Justice, on the other hand, seeks to foster the common good, promoting fairness and respect among individuals and communities. It challenges us to recognize the dignity of each person as created in the image of God, urging us to act in ways that uphold this truth. Practicing justice involves more than legalistic adherence; it demands a heart attuned to the cry of those who suffer, an unwavering commitment to equity, and a passion for truth.

Fortitude presents itself as the virtue of courage amidst trials and challenges. It strengthens our resolve to remain steadfast in faith when faced with adversities—whether personal struggles, societal pressures, or spiritual battles. Fortitude empowers young people to face fears that threaten their moral integrity and perseverance, encouraging them to pursue faith-filled lives without yielding to worldly distractions.

Temperance moderates our appetites and desires, ensuring we appreciate creation's gifts while not becoming enslaved by them. In the age of instant gratification and unrestrained consumption, temperance calls us to a life of balance and self-control. It invites us to reflect on the true purpose of our desires, reminding us that fulfillment arises not from excess, but from appreciation and gratitude.

Beyond these cardinal virtues, theological virtues of faith, hope, and charity impose an infusion of grace, guiding our relationship with God. Faith anchors us in truth, transcending mere belief to become a lived expression of trust. Hope sustains us amid life's uncertainties, assuring us of God's promise and presence. Charity, the greatest of all, compels us to love God and neighbor in radical, self-giving ways.

Identifying and embodying these virtues often requires the active participation of a supportive community. Here lies a special role for the Knights of Columbus and their educational mission. Through mentorship and example, the Knights provide a framework within which younger members can discern and cultivate virtues inherent in their identity as children of God.

To aid in this pursuit, it is beneficial to engage in regular self-reflection, with questions that probe the depth of our intentions and actions. Writing a journal, fostering a dialogue with God in prayer, or participating in spiritual direction are ways to clarify one's virtue-related aspirations and challenges. The process is not about self-perfection but about striving continually toward genuine conversion of heart.

Importantly, virtues do not develop in isolation. They intertwine and grow through practice and experience in daily life. Virtues are cultivated through choices—the way we respond to family, friends, and even strangers. Through each decision, we have the opportunity to live out the Gospel values in tangible ways, reinforcing the moral fabric of our lives.

The journey of identifying virtues continues until we meet our Creator in His eternal embrace. As such, it is a journey of hope and promise—rooted in the unyielding conviction that every step made in love and guided by virtue contributes to a more humane society and brings us nearer to God's kingdom.

Living out the virtues requires commitment, but it also promises immense spiritual and personal growth. While the task may seem daunting, remember that grace is abundantly provided to strengthen us along the way. Let us therefore embrace this challenge, confident in the guidance of the Holy Spirit, who continually renews us and works in us for our good and that of the world.

Exercises in Virtue Building

In a world brimming with distractions and challenges, developing virtues isn't just beneficial; it's crucial for living a life aligned with God's call. Virtue building, akin to exercising the body, demands commitment and practice. This is where we can draw inspiration from saints and faith heroes, whose lives were testaments to cultivated virtues. Drawing from their examples, we'll explore exercises that can shape us into better versions of ourselves, embracing the Theology of the Body in our daily lives.

One effective exercise in building virtue involves regular self-reflection. Taking a few moments each day to reflect upon our actions can be transformational. By examining our choices and motivations, we're given the opportunity to recognize where we've succeeded in living virtuously and where we've fallen short. This self-awareness is fundamental to growth. Journaling can be a helpful tool in this process, allowing for tangible insight into our spiritual journey.

Another essential practice is the cultivation of gratitude. A grateful heart is fertile ground for virtue. By actively counting blessings and expressing thanks, we shift our focus from what's lacking to what's abundant. This simple exercise can deter negative thoughts and foster a spirit of joy and generosity. As we grow in gratitude, we start to appreciate the goodness in others, leading to deeper, more meaningful relationships.

Prayer, the cornerstone of our faith, serves as both a conversation with God and an exercise in virtue. Through prayer, we align our will with His, seeking divine guidance in our efforts to be more virtuous. Incorporating prayers specifically aimed at growth in virtue—such as those seeking patience, humility, or charity—can powerfully fortify our resolve. Beyond formal prayer, inviting God into everyday moments enriches our lives with His presence and support.

Engaging in acts of service is a practical and powerful way to build virtues like compassion and empathy. Whether it's volunteering at a local shelter, assisting an elderly neighbor with their errands, or participating in Knights of Columbus charitable initiatives, these acts push us beyond ourselves. Selfless service teaches us to prioritize the needs of others, nurturing an other-centered mindset that aligns closely with Christ's teachings.

The power of mentorship can't be understated in virtue building. Guidance from those who walk the path of virtue provides insights and encouragement that books alone can't offer. A mentor, perhaps a Knight or community leader, can challenge us to set higher standards and offer wisdom when we face obstacles. In turn, being a mentor to someone younger creates a cycle of growth and accountability, spreading the practice of virtue throughout the community.

Practicing silence and mindfulness is another invaluable exercise. In today's fast-paced world, few of us make time to sit quietly and listen. Embracing silence allows us the tranquility needed to hear God's whispers in our hearts. Mindfulness, or living fully in the present, helps us appreciate each moment as a gift. These practices cultivate patience and temperance, virtues essential in navigating life's turbulences.

Reading lives of the saints provides not only inspiration but also practical examples of how to live virtuously. By studying how these holy men and women faced their struggles and grew in faith, we can adapt similar practices to our lives. They teach us that virtue isn't developed in isolation but through the ordinary occurrences of daily life. These stories serve as blueprints for developing courage, perseverance, and hope.

Community involvement plays a significant role in the journey of virtue building. Joining faith-based groups, attending retreats, or participating in Knights of Columbus activities strengthens our sense of belonging and accountability. In these settings, we're encouraged, supported, and sometimes challenged, all of which contribute to our growth. The sense of unity and shared purpose is a fertile ground for cultivating virtues such as respect and loyalty.

Setting personal goals for virtue cultivation can provide direction and motivation. Just as athletes set milestones, we're encouraged to outline clear, achievable objectives. Whether it's aiming to be more forgiving or striving to develop greater integrity, having a set goal keeps us focused and committed. These goals should be revisited regularly, measuring progress and adjusting as needed, fostering adaptability and perseverance.

Finally, embracing the sacrament of reconciliation is integral in the exercise of building virtues. It's a practice of humility, where we openly acknowledge our failings and experience God's endless mercy and forgiveness. This sacrament cleanses our soul, freeing us to start afresh. It's not just about seeking forgiveness but also about renewing our commitment to live a virtuous life, armed with the lessons learned from past errors.

Virtue building, much like any discipline, requires perseverance. It's a journey marked by stumbles and victories, yet each step draws us closer to the person God calls us to be. Through intentional practice and leaning into the vast riches of our faith, we can forge a life of holiness that not only enriches our own souls but also illuminates the world, reflecting God's boundless love and grace.

Chapter 16: Theology of Suffering

Suffering is an intrinsic part of the human experience, but within the Christian faith, it carries a profound significance that transcends mere hardship. As Roman Catholics, we are invited to unite our struggles with the redemptive suffering of Christ, finding purpose and hope amid pain. This chapter encourages young adults and teenagers to see suffering not as a burden to be feared but as an opportunity to deepen their faith and develop resilience in the face of life's trials. In understanding the theology of suffering, we learn to discover God's presence in the shadows of our difficulties, fostering a transformative encounter that can lead to spiritual maturity and a more profound communion with God. By embracing this path, the Knights of Columbus can guide the youth to recognize the hidden grace in suffering, cultivating a heart that seeks to love and forgive, drawing strength from the mystery of the Cross.

Redemptive Nature of Suffering

Too often, suffering is viewed through a lens of despair and hopelessness. Within the rich tradition of Catholic teachings, however, lies the profound understanding of suffering's redemptive nature. This perspective transforms our experiences of pain from mere trials to potential pathways that lead us closer to God's grace. In this section, we will explore how suffering isn't just a burden to bear but an opportunity for spiritual growth and redemption.

At the heart of this view is the life of Christ himself. Christ's passion and crucifixion symbolize the ultimate testimony of redemptive suffering. His journey wasn't one of avoidance or mere endurance; rather, it was an embrace of the divine plan. By his suffering, Jesus opened the doors to salvation, demonstrating that pain, when united with His, can have a purpose and value beyond our understanding. This profound mystery invites us to see our own suffering through this redemptive lens.

For Roman Catholics, especially young adults and teenagers, this concept might seem challenging. The idea that suffering can have meaning contradicts a world that often prioritizes comfort and success. Yet, understanding the redemptive nature of suffering aligns us with a deeper, more fulfilling spiritual reality. Through prayer, reflection, and the sacraments, we can begin to see our struggles not only as obstacles but as possible avenues for grace.

In practical terms, embracing the redemptive nature of suffering involves a conscious decision to unite our pain with Christ's own suffering. This doesn't mean seeking out hardship but rather finding meaning in the unavoidable trials life presents. Saint Paul talks about this in his letters, urging us to take part in Christ's sufferings so we may also share in His glory. Such unity with Christ through suffering requires faith and a heart open to God's mysteries.

Historically, many saints have exemplified this redemptive understanding of suffering. Take, for instance, Saint Maximilian Kolbe, whose martyrdom in a concentration camp stands as a testament to love and sacrifice. Offering his life in place of another, Kolbe transformed the horror of his suffering into an incredible act of self-giving love, echoing Christ's own sacrifice. His story inspires us to find holiness in suffering and see it as a call to deeper communion with God and others.

Furthermore, Saint Therese of Lisieux introduced the "Little Way," which suggests that even the smallest acts of love and acceptance in our struggles elevate them to redemptive significance. Her spirituality shows us that it's not the magnitude of our suffering that matters, but our response to it. With humility and trust, our daily burdens become offerings that draw us into the heart of Christ.

Recognizing the redemptive nature of suffering doesn't erase the pain—it sanctifies it. Integrating this understanding within Theology of the Body encourages teenagers and young adults to appreciate their innate dignity and purpose, even amidst trials. It instills resilience, empowering them to witness life's challenges as not just tests, but opportunities to participate in Christ's suffering and resurrection.

In family and community settings, this perspective alters how we perceive and support one another through hardships. With empathy and compassion, suffering becomes a shared journey. Families and communities that understand the redemptive nature of suffering can foster environments of mutual encouragement and hope. They become places where individual pain is not isolated but is transformed into collective strength through shared faith.

Instructionally, the Knights of Columbus play a pivotal role in disseminating these teachings. As leaders, they can guide young adults to find Christ in their suffering by exemplifying and teaching resilience rooted in faith. Programs and discussions that focus on the theology of suffering can provide a foundation for this journey, encouraging young people to offer their hardships in union with Christ as acts of love and sacrifice.

Moreover, understanding suffering's redemptive nature invites us into a deeper relationship with God. It enhances our prayer lives, moving us toward a spirituality that embraces both joy and sorrow. In prayer, we not only find solace but also the strength to offer our pain for the redemption of the world, a doctrine that remains central to Catholic belief.

To summarize, the redemptive nature of suffering within the Theology of the Body underscores the transformative power of pain embraced for a higher purpose. It aligns us with the ultimate act of love—Christ's sacrifice—and teaches us that our sufferings can become a source of profound spiritual enrichment. As we move forward, may we hold onto this truth, seeing each trial not as a hindrance, but as a step closer to the divine.

Finding God in Hardships

Throughout life, we inevitably encounter moments of profound difficulty, testing not only our resilience but also our faith. These hardships might feel like an insurmountable burden, yet within them lies an opportunity for deep spiritual growth. In this space, we discover something magnificent: the presence of God even in our most challenging times.

To find God amid suffering, we need to shift our perspective. It's like adjusting our eyes to see the light filtering through a dense forest. Often, when we're in pain or distress, our immediate reaction is to question or even doubt. Why me? Why now? It's a natural response. However, if we take a moment to pause and reflect, we start to see beyond the pain. This doesn't mean the suffering disappears, but we begin to perceive it as a conduit for divine grace.

Consider the lives of saints who faced unimaginable trials. Their stories serve as profound examples of trust and faith. They remind us that suffering isn't in vain; there's a redemptive quality in it. Saint John Paul II spoke extensively about suffering, teaching us that every human pain is an invitation to unite ourselves with Christ's sufferings. It's a reminder that our struggles have a purpose and can lead us towards redemption.

In times of hardship, prayer becomes a lifeline. It's not just a call for help but a conversation with God, a moment of intimacy where we bring our fears, hopes, and pains to Him. Through prayer, we slowly begin to understand that we are not alone in our struggles. God is there, providing us with strength and comfort, molding our hearts to be more aligned with His will.

Empathy, too, becomes crucial during these times. Within our communities, we can find solace in shared experiences. The Knights of Columbus, with their strong commitment to community and service, exemplify how collective support can lift individuals out of isolation. By sharing our stories and listening to others, we create an interconnectedness f faith, hope, and love that binds us together in Christ.

Moreover, it's essential to recognize that suffering helps us cultivate virtues we might not develop otherwise. Patience, compassion, humility—these can only grow through the trials that refine and strengthen our spirits. It's through adversity that we learn to love more deeply, forgive more readily, and persevere with greater courage.

There's also an element of mystery in suffering. While it's challenging to comprehend fully, we are reminded of Christ's sacrifice—the greatest act of love manifested through profound suffering. By contemplating His passion, we gain insight into the transformative power of hardships.

In these moments, we must rely on our faith. It's like an anchor that holds us steady when the storm rages around us. Trust that God's plan, though unfathomable at times, is ultimately one of hope and redemption. Each hardship is an invitation to draw closer to Him, to expand our understanding of His boundless love.

Finally, we learn to offer our suffering for others. It is a profound act of love to dedicate our own hardships for the good of another, much like Christ did for us. This self-giving teaches us the true nature of love and strengthens our bonds within the community of believers.

In every hardship, there lies the potential for transformation, for finding God in new and unexpected ways. Embrace the journey, knowing that through the depths of suffering, we can witness the heights of divine love, reshaping our lives and drawing us closer to the heart of God.

Chapter 17: Evangelization and Witness

Embarking on the journey of evangelization and witness invites us to become living testimonies of faith, where our actions speak louder than words ever could. In a world eager for authentic experiences, we are called to be the salt of the earth, seasoning our surroundings with the love of Christ through genuine acts of kindness and compassion. Sharing our faith stories isn't about grand speeches; it's about connecting with others in their struggles and joys, revealing how our lives intertwine with divine grace. This calling isn't reserved for the extraordinary moments but is found in the everyday tasks, the quiet contributions that ripple through our communities. As bearers of God's image, our witness becomes a beacon of hope, encouraging others, especially young adults and teenagers, to explore and embrace their own paths in the light of theological truths. In cultivating relationships that reflect Christ's love, we create spaces where true encounters with God can flourish, inspiring others to seek their own spiritual transformations. It's an ongoing mission where every interaction serves as an opportunity to spread the goodness we've experienced, fostering a vibrant community of faith anchored in the simple, yet profound acts of being present and being real.

Sharing Faith Stories

Stories have a profound impact on our hearts and minds. When it comes to evangelization, sharing personal faith stories acts like a powerful tool that can open doors to deeper understanding and connection. It's not just about telling tales; it's about communicating the lived experience of faith. In our journey as Catholics, the Knights of Columbus, young adults, and teenagers, we find ourselves not just bearers of tradition but also storytellers of the faith journey.

Imagine the power of a simple story about a moment when someone felt lost and God's love intervened. These narratives weave our lives into the grand revelation of the Gospel, bringing its timeless truths into the vividly personal arena of human experience. From a theological standpoint, sharing such stories contributes to building a communal identity, one where each believer sees their individual life reflecting a part of the divine narrative.

It's essential to remember that a well-told story cuts through cultural and generational barriers, reaching directly into the heart. Take, for instance, a teenager who recounts their struggle to maintain faith in a society driven by material success. By sharing this story, they not only offer a testimony of resilience but also provide a template that others might follow, encouraging them with the insight that they're not alone.

In crafting our faith narratives, authenticity is key. Real stories connect because they speak to the universal human experience—the highs, the lows, the moments of doubt, and the surprising instances of grace that catch us off guard. As we share, it becomes crucial to avoid embellishing or diluting our experiences to make them more palatable. Instead, honesty and vulnerability foster an environment where listeners feel safe to explore their questions and struggles.

Equally important is listening to the stories of others. The act of listening can be as transformative as sharing. When we engage with another's story, we're invited into their world, seeing through their eyes and understanding their journey through faith. By listening, we provide a mirror that reflects back the love and compassion of Christ, showing that each story matters.

It's helpful to think about the varied settings in which we can share our stories. From informal gatherings at home to more structured church meetings, each environment provides an opportunity to spread the seeds of faith. Consider how the Knights of Columbus organize community events where members are encouraged to share testimonies. These gatherings can create lasting impressions and foster a supportive community where young adults and teenagers feel their voices are valued.

We don't have to wait for grand occasions to share our faith. Everyday interactions—whether at school, work, or social gatherings—often provide the best opportunities to engage others. A casual conversation can turn into a meaningful discussion when we gently interweave our faith experiences into the topics at hand.

However, sharing faith stories isn't just about evangelizing to those outside the Church; it's also a way to keep our internal community vibrant and dynamic. For teenagers and young adults, hearing about the faith journeys of fellow parishioners or mentors can be incredibly affirming. These stories provide living proof of a faith that is active and alive, even in the face of modern-day challenges.

To encourage this within the Knights of Columbus, consider formal mentorship programs or small faith groups where members at different life stages can regularly meet and share. Such setups not only promulgate the exchange of stories but also edify and build up the body of Christ in the community.

The age-old techniques of storytelling hold immense value. Use vivid imagery, consider pacing, and allow pauses that let the message sink in. A well-told story invites reflection, arguably one of the most underrated aspects of faith development in youth and adults alike. When guiding others on how to share their stories, remind them of the centrality of Christ's example. He often used parables, simple stories with profound moral truths, to communicate complex theological concepts.

As a community, it's important to cultivate an atmosphere where faith stories are celebrated. Perhaps designate a 'Faith Sharing Month' where the focus is on sharing and listening to these transformative narratives within parishes or Knights chapters. This not only highlights the communal aspect of storytelling but also reinforces a culture of openness and spiritual growth.

In conclusion, sharing faith stories is a fundamental aspect of evangelization in our Catholic journey. Each story contributes to the ongoing conversation of faith, bridging the gap between generations and cultures, and enriching the community. Through authentic storytelling, listening, and creating intentional spaces for sharing, we allow God's work through our lives to shine brightly, beckoning others into the fold.

Being an Example for Others

In a world that often seems chaotic and unpredictable, the call to be an example for others is a grounding force. This call is not exclusive to great leaders or historical saints; it is an invitation extended to each of us. Evangelization and witness, profound forms of living out the Gospel, demand that we talk the talk and walk the walk. Our every action has the potential to inspire, teach, and transform.

Our conduct in everyday life can powerfully affect those around us. Whether it's a kind word to a stranger, patience in a long line, or honesty in difficult situations, these acts embed themselves in the fabric of social interactions. Teenagers and young adults, especially, are like mirrors reflecting their surroundings. As Knights of Columbus, young Catholics, or steadfast believers, let this image be one of Christ-like integrity and love.

Being an example does not mean achieving perfection, nor does it mean having all the answers. It means striving towards holiness, even in our imperfections. We rely on Christ's grace to transform our failures into testimonies. When we fall, our rising is what inspires others, showing them that with God's grace, we are capable of extraordinary resilience.

Everyday acts of love, no matter how small, bear witness to the teachings of the Theology of the Body. This profound connection between the physical and the spiritual was passionately explored by Pope Saint John Paul II. He encouraged us to understand that our bodies themselves can be a testimony to divine love. True evangelization occurs in the mundane, through actions that demonstrate the dignity and sacredness of the human person.

Our society rewards superficial achievements—a viral post, a fleeting moment of fame. Against this backdrop, we propose a different kind of status: one of spiritual depth and authenticity. The Theology of the Body teaches that our value is in our being, not our doing. By living this truth, we provide others with a deeper, more enduring perspective on life's purpose.

Imagine a home, a school, or a community center teeming with individuals committed to embodying Christ's love. Those spaces become sanctuaries of peace and joy. The young watch and learn, seeing the fruits of virtues like patience, humility, and charity. As they witness these virtues in action, they're drawn to emulate them, fostering a new generation equipped to carry the light forward.

Yet, being an example for others also requires discernment and courage. It is more than displaying virtues; it's about making tough choices when faced with moral dilemmas. Our faith teaches us to stand firm in the truth, even when it isn't popular. This requires courage, particularly for young adults bombarded by contrary values in media and peer influences. Demonstrating steadfast faith, even quietly, can redefine what is "normal" in a secular world.

Consider the role of mentorship. For Knights of Columbus, older members can enrich the lives of younger ones through guided conversations and shared experiences. A mentor has the unique opportunity to lead by example, steering young minds towards authentic living amidst societal pressures. These relationships serve as tangible expressions of brotherhood and exemplify the beauty of shared faith journeys.

To be an evangelical witness is also to prioritize relationships. People are more willing to embrace lessons from someone who genuinely cares about their well-being. Building rapport opens hearts and eyes to the transformative power of Christ's love. When our lives are joyful expressions of faith and community, others naturally want to become a part of it.

Let's not ignore the importance of forgiveness and understanding in our journey. The person who learns to forgive becomes a living testament to the power of redemption. Every time forgiveness replaces bitterness, it writes a story of hope and healing. It shows others that mercy is not a weakness but a profound strength that transforms relationships.

In our quest to be role models, developing virtues is essential. A virtue-driven life results in consistent conduct in line with our beliefs. Knights and young Christians should focus on virtues like fortitude, temperance, and charity, engaging in exercises that cultivate these traits. Virtue-based living becomes a map guiding us through life's complexities.

We must ground our efforts in prayer and meditation. A prayerful person is a beacon of peace, radiating an inner light that attracts others to the path of righteousness. Through prayer, we align our intentions with God's will, ensuring that our actions bear witness to His glory.

Peer influence, especially among the youth, can be daunting. Yet, it is possible to effectively navigate these waters by showing that faith-based decisions lead to more profound happiness and fulfillment. Personal growth blossoms when it is rooted in faith and love, offering a robust defense against pressures to conform to less virtuous paths. Walking confidently in faith inspires others to find similar courage within themselves.

In conclusion, the call to be an example for others resonates deeply within the heart of evangelization and witness. It requires a consistent commitment to upholding dignity and pursuing holiness. By living authentic Christian lives and embracing our roles as examples, we become catalysts for change, nurturing communities rich in faith and imbued with love. It's this transformation that echoes the heart of the Gospel and illuminates the path for future generations. Let us embrace this call with renewed fervor, assured in the knowledge that our efforts are not in vain.

Chapter 18: Theology of the Body and Technology

In a world where technology is interwoven with the fabric of daily life, harmonizing it with our understanding of the body's sacredness is paramount. John Paul II's Theology of the Body teaches us to view our physical form as a profound gift, and this perspective extends into our digital interactions. Rather than allowing technology to dictate our lives, we're called to exercise discernment, using it as a tool to foster genuine communion and growth in faith. By reflecting on how we consume media and engage online, we can ensure our digital footprint reflects our commitment to dignity, love, and responsibility. It's not just about managing screen time; it's about integrating our faith with modern reality, nurturing a healthy digital life that upholds the values we cherish. Through this lens, technology becomes an extension of our mission, a platform for evangelization where we bear witness to the truth of the human person—crafted in the divine image, destined for relationship, and called to a higher purpose.

Responsible Use of Technology

In our modern age, technology weaves through every aspect of our daily lives. Whether we're communicating with loved ones, working, or seeking entertainment, the digital world is ever-present. This presence offers immense potential for good but also demands a discerning approach from those who seek to live according to the principles of the Theology of the Body.

The Church teaches that every innovation ought to be scrutinized through the lens of how it impacts human dignity and the authentic flourishing of the person. It's not about rejecting technology; rather, it's about engaging with it responsibly. The stakes are high since technology can either enhance or endanger our understanding and expression of love, identity, and what it means to be human.

Picture the internet not as a vast ocean of isolated information but rather as a bustling public square. Here, the Knights of Columbus can gather young adults and teenagers to teach these principles, offering guidance on how to navigate with integrity. When online, are we acting as responsible stewards of creation, or are we being swept up in a tide that leads us away from authentic connection and self-giving love?

Technology's rapid advancement can sometimes outpace our ability to reflect on its moral implications. This is where the concept of responsible use becomes essential. We must ask ourselves: How does this influence our bodies, minds, and relationships? Technology should never diminish the person but should instead serve as a tool that upholds human dignity.

Sometimes, the allure of social media or the convenience of instant information can obscure our perception of the real world. It's crucial to remember that our bodies are temples, as mentioned in previous chapters. We can't let virtual interactions replace the tangible expressions of love that our Theology of the Body emphasizes. It's vital to prioritize face-to-face connections whenever possible and to invest in relationships that truly matter.

The Knights of Columbus are uniquely positioned to educate youth about these concepts. Through targeted programs and discussions, they can emphasize the importance of striking a balance—a healthy digital life. Encouraging moderation and mindful consumption of digital content can aid young people in discerning their vocation without technological distractions that cloud judgment.

Consider the time spent staring at screens and contrast that with time spent in prayer, in nature, or in service to others. These moments hold opportunities to encounter God more deeply and to foster the bonds that technology alone cannot build. We must use our digital tools in ways that reflect our values, promoting truth, beauty, and goodness while guarding against misuse.

Moreover, the Knights can play a pivotal role in helping young Catholics develop a critical eye when assessing the media. In a world where values are often distorted, and truth is subjective, this chapter aims to equip youth with the skill to filter out the noise. The aim is to uphold the dignity of the body and to love genuinely, even in digital realms.

As we integrate these practices into our digital engagement, we find a template for responsible use. Our online actions should act as witnesses to our beliefs, echoing the same virtues we strive to cultivate in all other areas of life. By remaining vigilant and intentional, we can transform technology from a distraction into a tool for evangelization and deeper relationship.

The Knights of Columbus, through their teachings, can illuminate the path whereby technology remains an instrument for good. They can foster environments where technology serves to expand our understanding of God's creation rather than restrict it. Our aim should always be to reflect the love, mercy, and truth of Christ online just as much as we do offline.

Ultimately, what we're striving for is the ability to witness our faith authentically, seamlessly blending our lives in both the tangible and digital realms. Only by using technology responsibly can we honor the God-given dignity that resides within us all. Thus, as this chapter unfolds, let it be a handbook for embracing the challenges and opportunities of the digital age with both courage and compassion.

Towards a Healthy Digital Life

The digital age offers countless opportunities but also presents significant challenges, especially for young Catholics striving to live out the teachings of Theology of the Body. Integrating faith with our online interactions is essential if we're to navigate this landscape with integrity and grace. As Pope Saint John Paul II emphasized, our bodies are not mere objects but rather temples of the Holy Spirit. This understanding should extend to our digital presence, where the lines between physical and virtual selves often blur.

Technology can be a double-edged sword. On one hand, it connects us with others, provides platforms for sharing faith, and even offers new ways to engage with spiritual practices. On the other hand, it can become an avenue for distraction, temptation, and the erosion of personal relationships. A healthy digital life demands discernment. It's not just about limiting screen time; it's about fostering meaningful connections and using technology as a tool to enrich our lives and the lives of others.

We can start by asking ourselves honest questions about our digital habits. Are they enhancing our ability to love and serve or pulling us away from these core purposes? Are we falling into the trap of comparison and envy, spending hours scrolling through carefully curated lives that chip away at our self-worth and dignity? This self-reflection helps us realign our digital behavior with our genuine identity as imago Dei—image of God.

In practical terms, setting boundaries is critical. Limiting social media use, focusing on producing rather than consuming, and prioritizing in-person interactions are all strategies that nurture a balanced approach. These choices empower us to engage with technology while remaining anchored in our values. Knights of Columbus, especially, can lead by example, demonstrating how to reconcile modern tools with ancient truths.

Pope Benedict XVI once remarked on the culture of silence—something increasingly rare in today's connected world. Embracing silence, even if just for a few moments each day, allows space for contemplation and for God's voice to be heard over the cacophony of the digital world. Incorporating moments of quiet into our daily routine offers a respite from noise, fostering a more profound connection with God.

While we're called to use technology, we're also called to witness to its Creator. This requires a proactive stance—engaging, not merely consuming. Online evangelization becomes an authentic expression of our mission. Sharing positive, faith-based content, engaging in prayers or discussions online, and supporting Catholic platforms are just a few ways to light a candle in the digital space.

But let's not overlook the importance of community. Digital tools should supplement, not replace, real-life interactions. Whether it's participating in parish activities, joining a Knights of Columbus council, or attending a retreat, these experiences ground us in a community of believers. They remind us we're part of something grander than our individual screens.

Young people, as digital natives, have a unique aptitude and understanding of technology. Yet, it's crucial for them to see it as a gift to be used wisely. Educational programs led by the Knights of Columbus can equip teenagers and young adults with skills to navigate digital realms responsibly. These programs should focus not only on technical literacy but also on ethical considerations, tying back to the ideals espoused in Theology of the Body.

Ultimately, a healthy digital life springs from a heart attuned to love and grounded in personal dignity. Everything we've been gifted—our bodies, our relationships, our abilities—can find new expression through technology. When we bring these expressions to God, offering our digital lives as part of our spiritual journey, we become witnesses to the truth that technology, too, can serve God's kingdom.

Chapter 19: Art and Theology of the Body

In this chapter, we explore the profound connection between art and the theology of the body, uncovering how artistic expression serves as a powerful vehicle for conveying the truths of our faith. From the rich history of sacred art to contemporary creations inspired by divine beauty, art invites us to ponder the mystery of the human person as an image of God. It is more than just aesthetic appreciation; it is a means of engaging with the divine. Through this lens, we see how the human body's depiction in art can echo the sacredness imbued in each of us, reminding us of our call to live in holiness. Sacred art can inspire contemplation and reflection, fostering a deeper understanding of our vocation to love and serve. Let art guide us in appreciating the divine message woven into the fabric of humanity, capturing the essence of the theology of the body in tangible forms that speak to the heart, and transcending cultural and temporal boundaries to unite us in faith.

Artistic Expression of Faith

Theology of the Body presents us with profound truths about our human experience. It beckons us to understand our existence and purpose through the lens of our faith in Christ. Integral to this pursuit is the ways we express faith through art, weaving strands of divine understanding into the fabric of our lives. Artistic expression of faith is not just about creating beautiful things; it's about communicating the beauty of God's love, His mysteries, and our own journey toward Him. This expression becomes a bridge connecting the earthly with the divine, allowing us to glimpse the eternal through fleeting moments of inspired creativity.

Art, in its many forms, has been a companion to faith throughout history, from the frescoes adorning cathedral ceilings to the serene melodies of sacred music echoing through church halls. Each brush stroke, each note, conveys more than just human skill. They convey an encounter with God, a manifestation of the divine touching the human spirit. For young people today, understanding art as a medium for theological reflection can be transformative. It empowers them to explore their spiritual questions and articulate their faith journey uniquely.

To integrate art as an expression of faith, one should appreciate that creativity stems from the Creator himself. We are made in the image of God, the ultimate artist, whose artistry is seen in the cosmos and within ourselves. Our talents and creativity are gifts that we're tasked with nurturing and expressing. Engaging in art with a faith perspective means acknowledging art's power to inspire, to teach, and to heal. It's a way to respond to God's call to participate in creation, recognizing our role as co-creators in a world that craves meaning and hope.

Imagine a canvas filled with the vibrant colors of creation—a reflection of Genesis painted by a young believer who feels the thrill of bringing Biblical stories to life. In the act of painting, there's a dialogue between the artist and Creator, a silent prayer transformed into a visual proclamation of faith. Similarly, through poetry and song, young voices can echo King David's psalms, offering praise, lament, or thanksgiving. Each word, each line scrawled or sung, is an offering, a testament to our reliance on and relationship with the divine.

Yet, artistic expressions of faith aren't confined to the boundaries of religious motifs or themes explicitly tied to scripture. They encompass the entirety of the human condition seen through the eyes of faith. A sculpture of a suffering Christ can resonate profoundly with someone wrestling with personal trials, resonating with their quest for redemption and new life. Meanwhile, a modern dance piece might communicate the freedom found in grace, the liberation that accompanies surrender to God's will.

In youth ministry, encouraging young people to engage in artistic endeavors can invigorate their spiritual lives. It offers them a safe space to process their experiences and emotions, especially amid the challenges of modern youth. In art, they find a sanctuary where faith can be explored and expressed authentically. Art workshops, guided gallery walks, or group projects on sacred themes could become invaluable tools for bringing abstract religious concepts to life, fostering a community where faithful living is creatively examined and enjoyed.

Art isn't just an expression; it's a conversation starter, a way to invite dialogue around deeply personal beliefs and cultural narratives. In appreciating sacred art—whether ancient icons or contemporary digital renderings—young Catholics can learn to see beyond the surface to the theological truths and historical contexts embedded within. Artistic communities, both physical and virtual, further expand these discussions, offering platforms where young believers can critique, create, and converse about the ways faith informs art and vice versa.

Moreover, the creation of art inspired by faith has the potential to break down barriers between individuals and communities. A mural depicting scenes of peace and reconciliation can promote dialogue in a fractured world. A song of hope composed in the spirit of unity can resonate across different cultures, languages, and backgrounds, harmonizing the Church's diverse members in a chorus of shared faith. In today's interconnected world, digital platforms can amplify these artistic expressions, sharing faith-infused messages on a global scale.

It's essential to recognize that the artistic expression of faith can aid in personal spiritual growth and mission work. When youth engagement with art nurtures their spirituality, it fuels their capacity to witness to their faith. Whether through creating or appreciating, art can lead to deeper reflections on character, motivations, and the divine presence in all creation. It becomes a catalyst for evangelization—evoking introspection and inspiring others through tangible manifestations of transcendent truths.

As we encourage young adults and teenagers to explore artistic expression within the framework of Theology of the Body, we affirm their God-given potential to make visible the invisible realities of faith. Their journey toward understanding God through art can help foster a rich and nuanced relationship with the Divine, leading to personal and communal transformation. In art, the beat of a drum, the curve of a sculpture, or the strokes of a painting echo the heartbeat of our Creator, calling us into deeper communion with Him and one another.

By cultivating an environment where artistic expression of faith thrives within the framework of Theology of the Body, we prepare the next generation of Knights of Columbus and young Catholics to be not only carriers of tradition but innovators of expression—rooted in faith and ever open to the new ways God calls us to witness His boundless love and mercy through the beautiful and powerful language of art.

Engaging with Sacred Art

Exploring the intersection of art and theology reveals a profound avenue for engaging with the mysteries of faith. Sacred art doesn't just decorate our places of worship; it serves as a tangible expression of divine truth, enhancing our understanding of the Theology of the Body. Through sacred art, the invisible becomes visible, the untouchable is made felt, and paradoxically, in its silent forms, art speaks volumes. It invites young adults and the faithful to immerse themselves in a dialogue that elevates the soul's longing to connect with God.

Consider the compelling imagery found in many of the world's grand cathedrals and humble chapels. The stained glass windows, the icons, and the frescoes form a narrative that awakens a sense of wonder and devotion. Each piece of art holds theological reflections that are intricately designed to be understood by not just the mind but also the heart. Whether it's Michelangelo's "Creation of Adam" or the quiet simplicity of a votive candle, sacred art can open a path to a deeper comprehension of human dignity and divine beauty, as articulated in the Theology of the Body.

The Theology of the Body reminds us that our bodies are not mere vessels but sacred temples of the Holy Spirit. Drawing parallels, sacred art also serves as a vessel, carrying and transmitting sacred truths. When young believers study and reflect on religious artworks, they're not just appreciating aesthetic beauty. They're stepping into a space of reverence and contemplation, where the human form is recognized as a reflection of divine splendor. The physical depiction of biblical events and holy figures invites the observer to see beyond the flesh into the sacredness of creation itself.

Teaching young Catholics and Knights of Columbus to engage with sacred art is pivotal for their faith journey. Facilitators should encourage them to spend time before these works, contemplating the stories they tell and the emotions they evoke. A piece of art might inspire guided reflections or serve as a backdrop for prayer, providing a serene setting for encountering God. It's in this stillness and focus that sacred art begins to reveal its layered meanings, inviting viewers to ponder their vocation to love and the sanctity embossed on the human body created in God's image.

Art, by its nature, communicates in ways that words often can't. This intrinsic characteristic of art makes it an invaluable educational tool, especially for the younger generations who are visually and kinesthetically inclined. Sacred art thus becomes a language, an alternative to the spoken or written word, communicating the teachings of the Church and the mystery of the Incarnation. It captures the essence of the Gospel and reflects it back to the viewer, often stirring an internal dialogue that compels personal and communal reflection.

Knights of Columbus, in their mission to educate and form adolescents and young adults, can use sacred art as a bridge connecting traditional teachings with contemporary expressions of faith. Art can break down complex theological concepts into accessible, relatable visuals. This foundation encourages participants to explore scriptural stories, be inspired by saints' lives, and deeply appreciate the sacramental grace exhibited in their own lives through their corporeality. To behold a painting, to read iconography, is to engage with a medium that transcends barriers of time, culture, and language.

Empathy must remain a cornerstone as we engage with sacred art. Art requires us to pause, reflect, and feel. Whether it's the sorrow etched into Mary's face at the foot of the cross or the joy radiating from the resurrected Christ, art evokes an emotional response. These emotions then marry with understanding, creating a holistic engagement with faith. Knowing the context and the story behind each piece enriches this engagement, making the art not just seen but experienced, felt, and lived. This emotive resonance helps those encountering challenges in faith or life, to find solace and answers.

To immerse oneself in sacred art is to undertake a pilgrimage of the senses, guided by divine spirit. This pilgrimage can lead to personal transformation, echoing the sentiment that art, much like faith, is often about discovery more than resolution. Participants are encouraged to engage art in a way that challenges, inspires, and questions. The resultant dialogue is just as valuable as the conclusion it seeks. When Knights mentor young adults in theology and faith, they can utilize art as both a tool and companion on this journey—reflecting beauty, truth, and goodness.

Incorporating art into theological exploration fosters a space where questions about human existence, purpose, and divine intent can be pondered deeply. It is through this engagement that young Catholics and Knights can become artisans themselves, shaping their lives to reflect the divine artistry of our Creator. As each art piece is unique, so is each individual's path toward understanding and living out the Theology of the Body. In fostering a connection to sacred art, you're nurturing a relationship that stretches beyond the immediate, touching the eternal.

Art isn't meant to sit idly on walls or in corners. It calls for interaction, inviting observers to participate in an ongoing conversation involving theology, philosophy, and personal spirituality. There's an inherent call for the Knights of Columbus to facilitate art-focused retreats or workshops, encouraging these conversations amongst participants who come from varied backgrounds and experiences. These gatherings can empower young adults and teenagers to evolve as individuals while collectively upholding and deepening the Catholic tradition.

In conclusion, engaging with sacred art offers an extraordinary means to connect with the Theology of the Body. It provides a tactile encounter with divine love and teaches us about the sacredness of our own humanity. By promoting and participating in this engagement, we nurture a community that values aesthetic beauty wrapped in theological richness, propelling young adults towards an authentic integration of faith into daily life. As the Knights of Columbus lead this charge, they unite artistic expression with divine purpose, advancing a fuller expression of Catholic identity in a modern world.

Chapter 20: Youth Ministry and Community

In our rapidly changing world, youth ministry stands as a beacon of hope, inviting young people to delve deeper into their faith while fostering a sense of belonging within their communities. By integrating the Theology of the Body into youth programs, we can inspire a holistic understanding of human dignity and vocation to love, empowering teens to navigate life's challenges with grace. It's not just about leading youth groups; it's about creating vibrant, faith-centered communities where young people can forge authentic relationships, grounded in love and respect. Here, the Knights of Columbus play a pivotal role in mentoring and guiding future leaders, ensuring that the spiritual flame remains alive through shared experiences and collective worship. By cultivating such environments, we help youth embrace their unique callings, encouraging them to become active participants in building a vibrant Church that celebrates the fullness of life. This mission requires patience, empathy, and a deep understanding of their struggles and aspirations, laying a solid foundation for lifelong faith journeys.

Building Strong Faith Communities

In today's fast-paced world, the young people within our church communities face countless challenges. They're juggling school, family, friendships, and the overwhelming influence of social media, often feeling pulled in a thousand directions. That's why building strong faith communities through youth ministry isn't just beneficial—it's essential. These communities offer a stable foundation where young people can nurture their faith, feel supported, and learn to embody the teachings of the Theology of the Body.

But how exactly do we go about building these communities? To start with, it requires an openness to engage and empathize with the specific needs and struggles of our youth. We need programs that don't just talk at them but speak with them. It's about creating spaces where dialogue is encouraged, where questions are welcomed, and where authentic relationships can grow.

Creating this kind of community starts with active listening. Youth leaders and Knights of Columbus must dedicate themselves to understanding the unique perspectives and challenges of each young individual. When youths feel heard, they're more likely to open up, participate, and grow in their faith. Our empathy becomes their trust, forming the bedrock of a faith community.

Beyond listening, there must be a structured approach to engaging activities that align with the Theology of the Body. These activities should be diverse: some might take the form of workshops where young adults can explore themes like love, responsibility, and understanding human dignity. Others could be service projects that align with the principles of charity and community service exemplified by the Knights of Columbus.

Including service activities not only enacts the principles of the Theology of the Body but also fosters a sense of purpose. When young people engage in acts of service, they're reminded of their intrinsic ability to impact the world positively, reinforcing their identity as valuable individuals made in the image of God.

Another vital component in building strong faith communities is mentorship. Knights of Columbus have a unique opportunity to serve as mentors, guiding young people through spiritual, personal, and moral development. By sharing their own stories and experiences, they can inspire and model what it means to live a life of faith and service. Mentorship creates bonds that are nurturing and enduring, fostering a sense of belonging that encourages young people to stay active within the church community.

Additionally, it's crucial to cultivate an environment rich in prayer and spiritual resources. Encourage young people to lead prayer sessions, meditations, or Bible study groups. By allowing them ownership over their spiritual journey, they learn to prioritize and integrate faith into their daily lives. The Sacraments, too, offer invaluable moments for deepening one's connection with God, and should be emphasized as vital components of community life.

One can't overlook the power of celebration and fellowship in fortifying a faith community. Regular gatherings, whether they're simple potlucks or grander events, foster unity. Sharing meals, enjoying each other's company, and engaging in meaningful conversations facilitate genuine friendships that stand the test of time.

The role of technology in building faith communities is an exciting frontier. Used wisely, digital platforms can supplement in-person gatherings, keeping the community connected beyond church walls. Creating digital groups where members can discuss, share insights, and support one another can transform how we build and nurture our communities.

Yet, while technology offers new opportunities, we must guide its use with intention and care, ensuring it enhances rather than detracts from real, human connections. Encouraging young people to balance digital and offline interactions can lead to a more authentic community experience.

Finally, adaptability is key. As our culture shifts, so too must our methods of engagement. What may work for one group or generation might not resonate with another. Staying open to new ideas, listening to feedback, and being willing to evolve are not just practical steps—they're acts of faith.

In building strong faith communities, all members of the church, from the youth to the leadership, must understand and embrace their role within the community. It's about collective responsibility and mutual support, where each person feels valued and encouraged to contribute. Such an approach can transform our church communities into vibrant, inviting places where faith isn't just a belief but a lived reality.

Organizing and Leading Youth Groups

In the vibrant tapestry of our faith community, organizing and leading youth groups stands as an essential thread. It is through these gatherings that young people can explore the depths of their faith, build lasting relationships, and grow in their understanding of the Gospel. The task of guiding these groups falls upon us, the entrusted leaders, who are called to serve with wisdom, creativity, and empathy.

The foundation of any successful youth group begins with a clear vision. As leaders, we must define the purpose of our gatherings. Is it to dive deeper into theological studies, engage in community service, or perhaps provide a safe space for open discussion? By identifying the group's goals, we set the stage for meaningful interactions and purposeful growth. This begins with active listening—a cornerstone of leadership in youth ministry. By understanding the needs and aspirations of our young members, we can tailor our approach and create an environment where everyone feels valued and encouraged to participate.

Effective planning is crucial in bringing a youth group's vision to life. This involves not only selecting relevant topics but also designing engaging activities that stimulate thought and discussion. Consider incorporating a mix of discussions, service projects, and social events to keep the program dynamic and inviting. Regularly incorporating Theology of the Body themes can enrich this experience, as these concepts resonate deeply with the challenges and questions many young people face today. Discussions around human dignity, relationships, and personal vocation offer powerful insights that illuminate God's loving design for their lives.

While planning sets the direction, maintaining flexibility is equally important. Youth groups are dynamic, often shifting with the interests and needs of their members. There will be times when a planned activity doesn't resonate, and that's okay. Being open to change demonstrates an understanding and respect for the participants' input, fostering a sense of community ownership and engagement.

Empathy plays a pivotal role in leadership within youth groups. To lead effectively, we must walk alongside our young members, understanding their struggles and triumphs. This requires patience and a willingness to engage in honest, heartfelt conversations. Many teenagers and young adults face pressures that may seem insurmountable, whether they be academic, social, or personal. Offering a listening ear and compassionate heart can make a significant impact, reminding them they are not alone in their journey.

Faith formation is a central goal of youth ministry. We are not merely planning social activities; we're helping to shape the spiritual foundation of future generations. This responsibility calls us to be well-rooted in our own faith, able to discuss and exemplify Catholic teachings authentically. Regular prayer, both personal and communal, provides the spiritual fuel needed to serve effectively. Incorporating moments of prayer, reflection, and sacramental life into group activities helps anchor meetings in Christ's love and guidance.

Leadership is not a solo endeavor. It involves building a team of committed individuals who share the vision and mission of the youth group. Encouraging older teens or young adults to take on leadership roles fosters a culture of responsibility and growth. These emerging leaders can offer peer insights and connections that adults might miss. Moreover, they bring energy and creativity, essential ingredients in capturing the attention of younger participants.

Communication is another key element in successfully organizing and leading youth groups. Clear, consistent communication with both group members and their parents establishes trust and sets expectations. Utilizing modern technology wisely, such as group messaging apps or social media platforms, can effectively keep everyone informed and ease the process of organizing activities. However, it is vital to model healthy boundaries with technology to ensure it enhances, rather than detracts from, the group's spiritual goals.

Service projects offer youth groups the opportunity to express their faith in action. These projects should align with the values of the Knights of Columbus, emphasizing charity, unity, and fraternity. Whether it's serving a local food bank, organizing a community clean-up, or visiting the elderly, these experiences provide tangible expressions of faith and a chance for young people to see the impact of their actions. Moreover, these projects often spark deeper discussions about the call to live out one's vocation in service to others.

One essential aspect of leading a youth group is the celebration of milestones and achievements. Recognizing individual and group accomplishments fosters a sense of belonging and enhances participants' sense of self-worth. This can be as simple as acknowledging personal growth in faith or celebrating the completion of a group service project. By celebrating these moments, we affirm the value of each member's contribution and strengthen the community bond.

Finally, leaders should continually seek opportunities for personal growth and development. Participating in workshops, attending retreats, or consulting with experienced mentors can vastly enrich one's ability to lead effectively. Leadership is a journey of lifelong learning, fueled by faith and a commitment to serve Christ through serving others.

To sum up, organizing and leading youth groups within the context of Roman Catholic teachings is a fulfilling and impactful endeavor. It requires a combination of vision, empathy, and dedication. Guided by the principles articulated through Theology of the Body, leaders can inspire young people to embrace their faith more deeply and grow in their journey toward holiness. Through vibrant activities, thoughtful discussions, and heartfelt service, youth group leaders nurture the seeds of faith planted by the Knights of Columbus and foster a community of engaged young Catholics ready to face the future with conviction and courage.

Chapter 21: Building a Culture of Life

In cultivating a culture of life, we're called to recognize and cherish the inherent dignity of every human being from conception to natural death. This chapter invites you to actively engage with the profound teachings of the Church, emphasizing the sanctity of life as central to the Theology of the Body. Embracing a pro-life stance involves more than just advocacy; it's about nurturing an environment where love and respect for all life flourish, mirroring God's unconditional love for humanity. By living out these convictions through daily actions and compassionate discourse, young Catholics and the Knights of Columbus can be powerful vessels for change in families, communities, and beyond. Together, guided by faith and bound by the strength of our convictions, we strive to embody these values, offering a radiant testament to the amalgam of hope, activism, and unwavering commitment to all God's children.

Pro-Life Teachings

Central to building a culture of life is understanding and embracing pro-life teachings. At the heart of these teachings is the acknowledgment of life as a sacred gift from God, deserving of reverence and protection from the moment of conception until natural death.

In today's society, where life is often undervalued or taken for granted, the call to uphold the dignity of every human person is more critical than ever. It requires a deep-seated respect for the inherent worth and potential of each individual. As Roman Catholics and Knights of Columbus, we carry the profound responsibility to champion this belief, ensuring that every life is cherished.

But what exactly does it mean to be pro-life? It's not merely about opposing abortion, though that's a significant part of it. It's about a consistent ethic of life—a commitment to safeguarding life in all its stages and conditions. This means advocating for the poor, the elderly, the sick, and the marginalized. It means standing against practices that diminish the value of life, such as euthanasia and the death penalty.

Pro-life teachings call us to see beyond our immediate experiences and biases. They demand empathy, urging us to walk in the shoes of those whose voices are easily drowned out or dismissed. For young adults and teenagers, this can be a powerful awakening—a chance to engage with the world empathetically and justly.

Consider the power of a single voice. In a world where technology allows our words to travel far and wide, the impact of standing up for life can be immense. As young Catholics, when we speak about the sanctity of life, we're not just echoing Church teachings; we're embodying them through action and example.

Educators and mentors in the Knights of Columbus bear the honor and task of guiding young hearts and minds towards these truths. They must cultivate an environment where questions are welcomed and where faith and reason go hand in hand. Thus, the classroom becomes not just a place of learning but a sanctuary where life is celebrated and defended.

The pro-life stance is rooted in love, which is perhaps the most transformative force. It calls us to love without conditions, without holding back. Envision every interaction and relationship as an opportunity to affirm life. That could be through small acts of kindness or larger efforts in advocacy and community involvement.

Our journey as defenders of life is not solitary. It's intertwined with the lives we seek to protect. Join forces with others through prayer, service, and pro-life actions, creating a network of support, understanding, and strength.

Building a culture of life also involves challenging societal norms and pressures that seek to commodify life. This means being fearless in pointing out the discrepancies between the truth the Church teaches and the messages that pervade the secular world.

For teenagers and young adults, these challenges are an invitation to discern, grow, and become leaders in their own right. Through formation programs and activities led by the Knights, they gain the tools needed to navigate these complex moral landscapes.

Ultimately, pro-life teachings encourage us to dream of a world where life is regarded with awe and gratitude. It's about inspiring a movement that transcends generations, where we pass on the torch of life's sacredness to those who come after us.

Let us be firm in hope and resilient in action, remembering that to be pro-life is to choose life in every possible sense—spiritually, emotionally, physically, and communally. Together, through courage and compassion, we can build a culture of life that reflects the love of our Creator.

Advocacy and Actions

In the pursuit of building a culture of life, advocacy and action are not just idealistic concepts but necessary responses to a call that resonates deeply within the heart of every believer. This call compels us to rise up and champion the values inherent in the Theology of the Body, where life is celebrated and protected in all its stages. It is through our advocacy and actions that we concretely express our dedication to the ideals that shape our faith and guide us towards a more compassionate world.

To begin, we must embrace advocacy as both a personal and communal endeavor. As individuals, this means educating ourselves on the Church's teachings. The rich doctrines surrounding life—especially as articulated through the Theology of the Body—provide a philosophical and theological framework that informs our actions. When we engage with these doctrines, we're not only reinforcing our understanding but also equipping ourselves with the tools to dialogue effectively with others.

At a communal level, the Knights of Columbus have long embodied the spirit of advocacy by mobilizing resources and organizing initiatives that uphold pro-life values. However, the challenge lies in ensuring that these efforts resonate with younger generations. Younger Catholics often seek to make an impact in a more global and interconnected world. Hence, leveraging technology and social media effectively can amplify our advocacy efforts, aligning them with how young people interact with information and engage in activism today.

Consider organizing workshops and training sessions tailored specifically for teenagers and young adults. These sessions can focus on crucial advocacy skills such as public speaking, persuasive writing, and digital campaigning. By doing so, we empower the youth to not only grasp the core tenets of the Theology of the Body but to also become adept advocates in their own right. Encouraging their participation in activities like letter-writing campaigns to legislators or volunteering at pregnancy support centers can provide practical experiences that nurture a pro-life ethic.

Engagement doesn't stop at advocacy; it seamlessly transitions into action. Action requires us to step out of our comfort zones and enter the arenas that need our attention. Whether it's through peaceful marches, community service projects, or even engaging in respectful dialogues with those who hold differing views, action is where advocacy takes tangible form. For young Catholics, participating in national pro-life events like the March for Life not only reinforces their beliefs but connects them with a larger community striving towards a common goal.

Nevertheless, actions must be accompanied by a heart of empathy and understanding. The Theology of the Body is as much about showing love and respect as it is about defending life. It's crucial to remember that engaging with those who are undecided or hold opposing views requires patience and empathy. Constructive dialogue rooted in understanding and compassion can often build bridges where division seems most apparent.

Moreover, engaging with art and culture can also be a profound way to advocate for a culture of life. The arts provide a universal language that can transcend verbal and cultural barriers, touching hearts in a way that pure rhetoric sometimes cannot. By supporting or creating artistic expressions that highlight the sanctity and beauty of life, we can communicate our values in impactful ways. Encouraging young artists within our faith community to express these themes through music, visual arts, or drama could foster a vibrant and persuasive movement.

Combining advocacy with tangible acts of service reinforces the communal bonds within the church and the larger community. It could be as simple as visiting the elderly, supporting new parents, or providing resources for those in need. Through these actions, the abstract concepts of the Theology of the Body find real-world applications that reflect Christ's teachings on love and compassion.

To uphold a culture of life, it also requires us to challenge societal norms and robustly defend the dignity of the human person, a concept deeply embedded in the Theology of the Body. Advocacy should extend to addressing systemic issues that compromise human dignity, such as poverty, access to healthcare, and education. These efforts, united with prayer and spiritual support, contribute to a holistic approach to life advocacy.

In conclusion, the intertwined nature of advocacy and action is essential in manifesting a culture of life that aligns with the Theology of the Body. Each effort, grounded in faith and love, contributes to nurturing an environment where the sanctity of life is honored and celebrated. Let us tirelessly work together, Knights of Columbus members, youth, and believers alike, in this sacred endeavor, transforming our fervent convictions into actions that echo the love and beauty of God's creation.

Chapter 22: Unlocking Potential through Faith

Faith, when embraced as a fundamental force in our lives, can unlock the hidden potential that God has instilled within each of us. It's more than just a beacon of hope; it's the lens through which we recognize our God-given talents and see our unique paths more clearly. This chapter guides you on how faith acts as a catalyst, encouraging you to set meaningful goals and strive relentlessly for excellence. As young Catholics and members of the Knights of Columbus, you are invited to explore how aligning your aspirations with your faith can propel you toward fulfilling your divine purpose. Engaging with faith doesn't mean ignoring challenges but rather facing them with the conviction that you're not alone—God accompanies you in your journey. So, harness the strength of your faith and allow it to illuminate the possibilities that lie ahead, empowering you to become not only the architect of your destiny but also a beacon for others in this shared voyage towards holiness and purpose.

Recognizing God-Given Talents

In a world where we're often defined by external achievements and status, it's easy to overlook the unique gifts we each possess. Talents bestowed upon us by God are like seeds, waiting to be nurtured and cultivated into something magnificent. These are gifts meant not just for our benefit, but for the world. Have you ever considered what makes you truly unique? Let's delve into how the light of faith illuminates our special talents.

First, understanding that every talent is God-given places these abilities in a perspective that transcends mere personal gain. Our talents become vehicles of service, reflecting the divine creativity that crafted us in His image. Through the lens of faith, we begin to see ourselves not just as individuals with skills but as integral parts of a divine plan. This means that recognizing and honing these talents is not only beneficial but a profound act of participation in God's work.

The process of discovering these gifts can sometimes be daunting. It's not merely about identifying what we're good at, but discerning what brings us joy, what aligns with our values, and where we feel a deep sense of connection and purpose. This search often requires quiet reflection and prayer, allowing God to reveal His intentions for our gifts.

This introspective journey can be enlightening. For young adults and teenagers, particularly those on the path of Catholic formation, the interplay between self-discovery and faith is crucial. Consider how different your choices would be if every decision passed through this divine filter. Such a practice could illuminate paths that weren't visible before, directing your talents towards their truest potential.

As we recognize these talents, let's also recognize the call to courage and humility. Courage to step forward and embrace these gifts, even when the world might not fully understand their value. Humility to accept that these talents are not exclusively self-made; they're bestowed, and it is our responsibility to use them wisely.

The Knights of Columbus play a pivotal role here. By encouraging young adults to explore and hone their talents, they foster environments where these gifts can emerge and flourish. This aligns closely with their mission to build a stronger community grounded in faith and service. Furthermore, programs that highlight these talents through workshops, mentorships, and communal activities empower individuals to not only recognize their gifts but how to apply them constructively.

Imagine a world where every individual recognizes their unique talents and feels compelled to use them for the greater good. This vision aligns with the apostolic mission of the Church. It's a call to transform societies by living out our vocations authentically and passionately, powered by grace and truth.

One of the first steps in this transformation is to celebrate the small victories. Recognizing God-given talents doesn't always mean discovering grandiose abilities. Sometimes it's in the gentle strength of a listening ear, the perseverance of a dedicated worker, or the kind smile that provides solace in times of need. In acknowledging these seemingly modest talents, we profess the inherent dignity found in all vocations.

In practice, recognizing these talents requires intentional living. It involves asking ourselves key questions: What moves my heart? Where do I feel God's pleasure in my actions? What am I willing to practice and craft over time? Take heart in knowing that every moment of struggle, growth, and learning is shaping the talents God has entrusted you with. It is a labor of love, carried out through faith.

Developing these talents is often likened to a pilgrimage—a journey defined by faith, with many opportunities for reflection and refinement. At times, the path may be obscured by doubt or distraction, but the sacraments provide a compass to realign and reinvigorate us. Through the Eucharist, we draw strength; in confession, we find clarity, and in community, we find support.

In our contemporary culture, where digital distractions are pervasive, it's essential to carve out time and space to truly engage with these introspections. Encouraging young people to unplug, even for short periods, can be transformative. Allow the quietude of nature, the tranquility of sacred spaces, and the contemplative practice of prayer to become the backdrop against which these talents shine most brightly.

Moreover, sharing our talents with others ignites a reciprocal exchange—a cycle of generosity and gratitude. Whether it's through volunteering, mentoring, or simply sharing experiences, gifts once hidden can become obvious testimonies of God's love in action. This shared expression not only strengthens individual faith but reinforces communal bonds.

With the right blend of patience, perseverance, and prayer, we can cultivate an awareness that each of us is a vital thread in the fabric of our faith communities. As Roman Catholics and members of the Knights of Columbus, our mission becomes a shared journey, urging one another on toward the fulfillment of our God-given potential. In responding positively to this call, we do more than recognize our talents—we celebrate the manifold ways we can glorify God through them.

In closing, remember that you are uniquely crafted and called. Every talent, no matter how small it may seem, holds the potential for greatness. As you continue to embrace and develop these gifts, let your journey be guided by love, faith, and immeasurable grace. Indeed, the discovery and nurturing of your talents not only unlocks personal potential but opens pathways for you to contribute profoundly to the world around you.

Setting Goals and Striving for Excellence

In the journey of unlocking potential through faith, setting meaningful goals and striving for excellence become foundational pillars. Rooted in the understanding that each of us is created in the image of God, setting goals allows us to harness our God-given talents and channel them towards a higher purpose. It becomes a spiritual endeavor grounded in a desire to reflect the Creator's love and wisdom in all that we undertake.

First, it's important to recognize that setting goals is an act of alignment with God's will. When we align our personal aspirations with the teachings of the Church and the example of Christ, our goals are no longer just personal milestones. Instead, they become opportunities to serve God and others. This conscious act of alignment transforms the way we perceive success and excellence, as they are measured not merely by worldly standards but by how they reflect our commitment to our faith and community.

Consider the story of the loaves and fishes, where a seemingly small offering was transformed into a miracle. Our aspirations, no matter how modest they seem, can be multiplied when aligned with God's purposes. By striving for excellence in our endeavors, we're not just seeking personal achievement but participating in God's work to uplift and transform the world around us, starting with our immediate community.

The practice of setting goals must be approached with a heart open to divine guidance. Prayer and meditation act as crucial tools that help discern God's plan for us in our personal and professional lives. Through prayerful reflection, we can identify our strengths, weaknesses, and the unique ways we can contribute to building the Kingdom of God. It's during these quiet moments with God that we gain clarity and the courage to pursue our goals with faith and determination.

Once goals are set, perseverance becomes essential. The path to excellence, as illuminated by faith, is rarely easy or straightforward. It requires resilience, patience, and the fortitude to endure challenges and setbacks. Reflecting upon the perseverance of the Saints can be a powerful source of inspiration. Their unwavering commitment to their calling, despite immense trials, serves as a model for how we can steadfastly pursue our own God-given missions.

Importantly, as we strive for excellence, we must remember the significance of community and collaboration. The Knights of Columbus exemplify how communal support and shared values can nurture individual success. By encouraging one another and holding each other accountable, communities of faith foster environments where personal and communal goals can be pursued wholeheartedly. These communal bonds are crucial as they remind us that we are not journeying alone.

Moreover, striving for excellence involves embracing a spirit of humility. It's crucial to remember that our achievements are not solely the result of personal effort but are possible through God's grace and the support of others. This humility fosters gratitude and a readiness to give back, transforming successes into opportunities for service. By sharing our gifts and talents, we contribute to the greater good and reflect the love and generosity of Christ.

Young Catholics are especially called to courageously pursue their God-given missions with fervor and dedication. In a world that often presents conflicting messages about success and achievement, it's vital to ground their pursuits in the rich teachings of the Catholic faith. The Theology of the Body provides a framework that upholds the dignity of the human person and calls for a life that reflects God's truth and purity. By drawing from this, young adults can maintain a holistic view of success that includes personal, spiritual, and communal growth.

Practically, setting goals should be accompanied by action plans that are realistic, specific, and reflect personal values. Goals should be measured not only by the outcomes but by the virtue cultivated through their pursuit. This virtue-driven approach ensures that the journey is as significant as the destination, providing opportunities for growth in faith, character, and understanding.

In conclusion, the journey of setting goals and striving for excellence is an integral part of unlocking one's potential through faith. By aligning our goals with divine guidance, persevering through challenges, supporting one another in community, and maintaining humility and gratitude, we honor the God who has equipped us with unique talents and the capacity for greatness. Let us pursue excellence with love and dedication, knowing that in doing so, we glorify God in all things.

Chapter 23: Role of the Sacraments

The sacraments serve as profound channels of grace, bridging the divine and human realms in a way that nurtures the soul and fortifies our Catholic faith. Each sacrament acts as a beacon, illuminating our path toward holiness and the fullness of life in Christ. By participating in these holy rites, we are invited into a deeper communion with God and each other, reinforcing our commitment to the Church's mission. This transformative encounter fosters an enduring growth in love and understanding, urging us to not only receive but also embody the living presence of Christ. For young Catholics, especially Knights of Columbus, the sacraments offer an unshakeable foundation, crafting a rich monument of love, sacrifice, and renewal that reflects our sacred dignity as children of God, called to radiant fidelity and service in the world.

The Sacraments as Grace

The sacraments are not merely ritualistic acts, but profound incarnations of grace. Through them, God's presence becomes tangible, offering an encounter that's life-transforming and deeply personal. Each sacrament is a channel, a magnificent pathway through which divine grace flows into our lives, altering our very being from within and equipping us for the journey of faith. For young adults and teenagers, recognizing sacraments as grace is crucial; it transforms ordinary experiences into extraordinary moments of growth, connection, and understanding.

Pope Saint John Paul II spoke extensively about how the body's sacramentality reveals the mystery of grace. The sacraments, he taught, marry the spiritual and physical, demonstrating God's desire to be near us, dwell amongst us, and work through us. They are not distant or abstract concepts. Instead, they're deeply embedded in the human experience, mirroring our quest for love, truth, and purpose. This perspective invites us to see the sacraments as more than obligations—they are immersive rites that sustain our spiritual lives and affirm our identity as God's beloved children.

Consider baptism, the first sacrament of initiation. It is not just a ceremonial welcoming into the Christian community but an intimate encounter where one is cleansed of original sin and reborn into new life with Christ. The grace received here is foundational, inscribing in us a character that marks our souls for eternity. It calls us to live as part of a broader spiritual family, urging us to carry the light of Christ into the world.

Then there's the Eucharist, the heart and summit of Christian life. To partake in the Eucharist is to receive Christ himself—body, blood, soul, and divinity. This sacrament of love not only provides spiritual nourishment but also unites us more closely to Jesus and to each other as members of the Church. The grace found in the Eucharist is transformative; it empowers us to love as Christ loves, to forgive as he forgives, and to serve as he serves.

The sacrament of confirmation strengthens us with the Holy Spirit's gifts, echoing the apostles' Pentecostal experience. In a world that often challenges faith, especially for young adults and teenagers, confirmation offers a renewing grace that breathes courage into our hearts. It instills the strength needed to bear witness to Christ in our daily lives, transforming us into soldiers of faith, ready to engage with the complexities of the modern world.

Reconciling with God through the sacrament of penance brings forth a grace that heals the soul. In confession, we experience the mercy of God, who waits with open arms to forgive and restore us. Many youths struggle with the concept of forgiveness—not just forgiving others but accepting forgiveness for themselves. The grace of penance is liberating; it renews our relationship with God, encouraging us to rise from our failures with renewed hope.

Within the sacrament of matrimony, grace is ever abundant. For those called to this vocation, marriage is not merely a contract but a covenant, a holy commitment where two lives become one in a mystical union blessed by God. The grace of matrimony equips couples to build families rooted in love, respect, and faith. It turns everyday familial challenges into opportunities for growth and mutual sanctification, reflecting the unconditional love God has for his Church.

The anointing of the sick is a testament to God's profound compassion. It is through this sacrament that the grace of healing, whether physical, emotional, or spiritual, is given. This sacrament brings comfort to those in pain, opening their hearts to God's mysterious yet caring embrace. It reminds us all, especially the youth, of the ever-present hope and solace we find in trusting God's plan even amidst suffering.

The sacrament of holy orders confers grace upon those men chosen to serve the Church as deacons, priests, or bishops. The mission of ordained ministers is nothing less than the continuation of Christ's priestly work on earth. Through this unique grace, they are empowered to shepherd the faithful, administer other sacraments, and bear a distinctive witness to the Gospel. Their vocation serves as a beacon for youth, highlighting the diverse ways in which one can dedicate oneself to God's service.

Understanding sacraments as grace thus opens a window to a richer faith experience. Young people, in particular, find in them an anchor in contemporary society's shifting sands. Embracing this dynamic relationship challenges them to reflect on their identities not just as followers but as active participants in the Church's mission. They are called to recognize the sacredness of their bodies as temples of the Holy Spirit and conduits of divine grace.

In the sacramental life, we discover that grace does not simply equip us for occasional acts of virtue but cultivates in us a habitual disposition towards holiness. This consistent nurture and growth in grace is what John Paul II and other spiritual giants advocate. They challenge us to view each sacramental encounter not as isolated acts but as continuous invitations into deeper communion with the Triune God.

For teenagers and young adults, engaging with the sacraments is a stepping stone towards maturity in faith. It provides them not only spiritual sustenance but also the wisdom to navigate life's complex moral landscapes. By seeing sacraments as gifts of grace, they can cultivate a spirituality that is both resilient and responsive, one that sustains them through trials and triumphs alike.

The role of the sacraments as grace is not to be underestimated or misunderstood as mere symbolic gestures. They knit the material and immaterial, drawing the invisible into the visible realm of our existence. As the Knights of Columbus strive to develop a Theology of the Body curriculum, incorporating this understanding ensures that the youth grasp the profound truth that grace is not a distant promise but a present reality, accessible through the sacraments that shape the very essence of Christian life.

Participation in the Church

In the grand exercise of Catholic life, the sacraments are threads that bind us, drawing us closer to God and to one another. They invite us to deepen our participation in the Church, transforming ordinary moments into encounters with the divine. Understanding the role these sacred rites play in our lives reveals how intertwined our spiritual journeys are with the community of believers around us. Recognizing this connection is particularly vital for young adults and teenagers as they navigate their paths within the faith.

Participation in the Church through the sacraments isn't merely about adherence to rituals. It's about embracing a way of life that celebrates our identity as members of the Body of Christ. Each sacrament is a step on a journey toward living a holy and fulfilling life. The Knights of Columbus, with their dedication to fostering faith among young people, are perfectly positioned to guide this understanding. Their role as mentors can help illustrate how participation in these rituals is a cornerstone of Catholic identity and communal life.

Through Baptism, we enter into the Church, becoming part of a rich communal history that stretches back to Christ himself. This sacrament marks the start of our Christian life and initiates a relationship with other believers. Confirmation strengthens this bond by affirming our commitment to the Church and its teachings. As young members of the Church, understanding this connection can empower teenagers to see themselves as active participants, capable of making a meaningful impact within their communities.

The Eucharist, often called the "source and summit of Christian life," offers the most profound participation in the Church. In partaking of the Eucharist, we're united with Christ and his sacrifice. For young people, this sacrament serves as a reminder of the communal nature of worship and the importance of gathering together to celebrate our faith. It's here that the mystery of our faith is most tangibly experienced, grounding us in a spiritual reality that transcends the day-to-day.

Confession, also known as Reconciliation, restores our relationship with God and, by extension, our place in the Church. This sacrament is a powerful exercise in humility and grace, teaching us about mercy and forgiveness. By participating in Reconciliation, young Catholics learn valuable lessons about contrition and conversion, which are essential for personal growth and maintaining a healthy community dynamic.

For teens and young adults, the sacraments are gateways to greater involvement in the spiritual and communal life of the Church. In the teen years, moral and educational guidance becomes crucial, and the faith-driven support of an organization like the Knights of Columbus can help direct their journey. By organizing retreats, workshops, and study sessions around the sacraments, the Knights can offer spaces where young people explore their faith deeply, alongside peers and mentors.

The sacraments of Matrimony and Holy Orders offer unique participatory experiences, each with specific vocations in mind. They serve as reminders that every path we choose within the

Church is sacred, and every choice is a step on the journey of love and service. Understanding these sacraments fosters not just personal commitment but also an awareness of the broader mission: to emulate Christ in bringing love and mercy into the world.

Incorporating sacraments into regular engagement with Church life encourages young Catholics to see themselves as integral parts of the Catholic mission. The communal aspect of sacramental life inspires service and advocacy, driving action toward building a culture of life and compassion as taught by the Church. This participation promotes an active faith that is relevant and resonant in today's world, allowing young Catholics to internalize and express their beliefs authentically.

The role of the Knights of Columbus, in this context, becomes one of facilitation and accompaniment. By acting as guides and examples of lived faith, they illustrate the power of the sacraments in shaping and enhancing our lives. Through their initiatives, they can create opportunities for young adults to practice their faith in tangible ways, such as through community service that embodies Catholic social teachings.

Finally, participation in the Church through the sacraments brings us closer to Jesus and aligns our lives with his teachings. As Pope Saint John Paul II emphasized, understanding and living out the sacraments helps us recognize our bodies as sacraments themselves, visible signs of God's presence in the world. Engaging actively with the Church enhances this realization, nurturing a spirituality that acknowledges the divine in daily life and manifests God's love in every interaction.

In committing to the sacramental life, we commit to a lifelong journey of faith, steady in the challenges it presents and vibrant with the life it imparts. As part of this pilgrimage, each sacrament serves as a wellspring of grace and a source of strength. By cultivating a sincere participation in Church life, teenagers and young adults can tap into this divine grace, forging a path marked by love, service, and a true sense of belonging within the Catholic community.

Chapter 24: Embracing Diversity

In our journey toward understanding the Theology of the Body, we uncover the profound truth that diversity enriches our shared faith. The Knights of Columbus, with their commitment to fostering unity, remind us that embracing diversity isn't just about acknowledging differences, but celebrating them as reflections of God's boundless creativity. Our unique cultures and backgrounds weave a quilt that illustrates the universality of God's love—a love that transcends language, customs, and traditions. By recognizing and valuing diverse expressions of faith, we become more compassionate and empathetic, drawn closer not only to one another but to the very essence of humanity created in the image of God. In doing so, we create a more inclusive Church that resonates with the vibrant energy of its members, bound together in the spirit of love and understanding. Thus, as we embrace diversity, we learn to see each other with the eyes of Christ, fostering an environment where everyone can grow in faith and contribute their God-given gifts to the collective mission.

Unity in Diversity

In the heart of every community, especially those bonded by faith, lies the profound truth that unity does not demand uniformity. "Unity in Diversity," as it pertains within the context of our spirituality, invites us to explore the vibrant nature of human expression under one guiding light: the love of Christ. This awareness calls us to embrace differences while pursuing a deeper common bond, which is our shared identity as children of God.

This concept is especially poignant for us Roman Catholics, for whom the universal Church represents a mosaic of cultures, languages, and traditions. Our faith tradition is not a melting pot aiming to erase distinctions; rather, it's a mosaic, each unique piece contributing to the overall beauty. It's in this diversity that we can find richness, growing stronger through the collective experience of myriad cultures and perspectives.

The Knights of Columbus, as a worldwide fraternity, embody this diversity in their global reach. Their mission stands as a testament to the strength found in variety, proving that together, varied cultures and outlooks can enhance our witness to the Gospel. As Knights, and members of the Catholic community, we are called to live out this unity in diversity, cultivating our distinct gifts for the good of the whole.

Our journey begins with recognizing that every person carries the imprint of divine creation. Theology of the Body teaches us that we're made in the image and likeness of God, each presenting unique aspects of His love and wisdom. When we look at each other through this lens, we see not just differences, but the image of God reflected in our diversity. Pope Saint John Paul II, in his reflections on the Theology of the Body, illuminated how the human body is a manifestation of the spirit, a place where eternity and temporality meet. This understanding transcends cultural boundaries, uniting us in the acknowledgment of our shared humanity.

Consider the richness of a symphony, where each instrument contributes its individual sound to create a harmonious piece. Likewise, when different cultural expressions of faith come together, they create a symphony of praise to the Creator. Within our young adult and teenage communities, this diversity can be a source of learning and growth. Instead of viewing differences as barriers, they become opportunities for dialogue and deeper understanding.

Building unity requires effort and intentionality. It demands that we listen to one another, fostering mutual respect and admiration for the ways God's image is reflected in each person. This means stepping outside of comfort zones and being open to experiences and traditions different from our own. Such encounters not only enrich our personal lives but also reinforce our collective mission as a Church.

It's important to remember that unity doesn't negate individuality. Instead, it celebrates who each of us is, while inviting us to contribute toward a common goal. Young people, particularly, should be encouraged to explore how their personal gifts and cultural backgrounds can be harmoniously integrated into the broader faith community. This process can ignite a deeper commitment to living out their faith actively and authentically.

The concept of "Unity in Diversity" urges us to consider how we engage with those who are different from us. It questions how open we are to learning from others, listening to their stories, and recognizing their gifts. It's not an invitation to blend into homogeneity, but rather to celebrate and uphold the distinctive voices that contribute to the Church's mission.

In practical terms, the Knights of Columbus can serve as a powerful instrument for fostering this unity. Through their work in local communities and philanthropic activities, they create spaces where diverse groups can come together, advocating for common causes while respecting individual differences. This approach not only strengthens community bonds but also serves as a visible testament to the transformative power of unity in diversity.

By embracing this principle, young adults and teenagers can become catalysts for change within their own circles. As they navigate a world where divisions often overshadow commonalities, they are presented with the opportunity to be peacemakers, bridge-builders, and champions of inclusive love. The path of unity is not without its challenges, but it is through these trials that we may grow more resilient in our convictions and richer in spirit.

In conclusion, "Unity in Diversity" is more than a concept; it's a call to action and an embodiment of who we are as followers of Christ. By bringing together our varied experiences, we don't just coexist—we build the Kingdom of God on earth. When each unique identity is celebrated, we echo the harmony of a diverse, yet unified, Church, offering a powerful, hopeful witness to the world. So let us embrace our differences, learning from each other and growing together, recognizing that in this unity dwells the true strength of our community in faith.

Celebrating Different Cultures in Faith

As we explore the rich experience of human life through the lens of faith, we find that the call to embrace diversity resonates deeply within us. In our quest to understand the Theology of the Body and its application to our lives, recognizing the myriad ways God expresses Himself through diverse cultures becomes an essential journey. Each culture, with its unique customs, traditions, and expressions of faith, offers a distinct lens through which to witness the beauty of God's creation.

The Catholic Church has long celebrated its universality, inviting people from every nation, race, and tongue to unite in faith. This unity in diversity is not just an ideal; it's a lived experience of the Catholic community worldwide. It's in the embrace of a global Church that we meet brothers and sisters whose ways of worship and cultural heritage enrich and expand our perspective of faith. Each culture contributes its artistry, language, and worldview to the mosaic of our shared Catholic identity.

Understanding the significance of different cultures in faith involves entering a dialogue of hearts. In these interactions, we not only learn about others but also reflect on our own practices and beliefs. This exchange is essential in cultivating empathy and compassion, grounding us in the understanding that, despite varied outward appearances, our inner lives share the same yearning for God and the eternal.

Take, for instance, the vibrant expressions of Catholicism found in Latin American countries, where rituals and traditions are steeped in vivid celebrations such as the Day of the Dead or the colorful parades of holy processions. These festivities embody a faith lived joyfully and openly, connecting the sacred with the everyday in ways that leave indelible marks on community life. It's in learning from these practices that young people — especially within organizations like the Knights of Columbus — are prepared to appreciate and respect diverse cultural expressions within parishes and beyond.

Moreover, exploring African Christianity reveals a profound intertwining of faith and daily life, where worship often includes exuberant music, dance, and communal participation. These cultural elements not only serve as modes of expression but also unify communities in shared spiritual experiences. By witnessing and participating in these traditions, young Catholics can gain insights into the diverse ways in which Christ's message of love and hope is lived around the world.

In Asia, the silent reverence and deep meditation practices offer lessons in the art of stillness and contemplation. Cultures with rich traditions of prayer and reflection, such as those in the Indian subcontinent and the Far East, remind us of the value of silence in a world often filled with noise. Embracing such practices can deepen the prayer lives of teenagers and young adults, who might otherwise be engulfed by the frenetic pace of modern living.

Incorporating these cultural perspectives into a Theology of the Body curriculum involves creating spaces for dialogue, where young individuals are encouraged to share and learn from one another's cultural backgrounds. It means facilitating encounters that break down stereotypes and promote genuine understanding. Educators and mentors play a crucial role here, guiding discussions that not only celebrate cultural differences but also focus on the core truths that bind us as Catholics.

Furthermore, engaging with diverse cultures in faith is not a mere academic exercise but a living theology. It's about taking the lessons learned from cultural appreciation and applying them to real-world challenges, such as combating prejudice and fostering inclusion within our communities. Encouraging young people to be culturally aware and sensitive leaders helps create environments in which every person feels valued and loved.

At the heart of this journey lies the understanding that diversity, when approached with open hearts and minds, doesn't divide us but builds a richer, more complete picture of God's love. Each culture carries its gifts, contributed to the whole body of Christ, so the individual beauty of each part enlivens the entire Church.

This call to celebrate diversity is echoed powerfully within the Knights of Columbus, whose mission includes social upliftment, charitable actions, and fraternal unity. By integrating cultural appreciation into their programs, they equip young Catholics to see beyond borders and stand as ambassadors of unity in the world. This mission aligns seamlessly with the task of preparing future generations to live out the Theology of the Body, recognizing that our diverse cultural expressions are integral to our identity as images of God.

In conclusion, celebrating different cultures in faith is a vital chapter in our understanding of what it means to live as the Body of Christ. It's an invitation to honor not only the distinct traditions but also the shared humanity that reflects the divine. As we embrace this diversity, let us do so with the certitude that it brings us closer to the Kingdom of God, where every nation and culture contributes to the eternal choir of praise.

Chapter 25: Leadership and the Knights of Columbus

In the rich tradition of the Knights of Columbus, leadership is not merely about guiding others—it's about embodying faith and courage to inspire transformation in oneself and the community. For young Catholics delving into the Theology of the Body, these leadership skills are more than organizational tools; they're deeply rooted in a sincere commitment to live and love as Christ taught. The Knights stand as a testament to leading with integrity, nurturing a spirit of fraternity that echoes the Church's call to unity and compassion. By cultivating virtues of humility, service, and steadfastness, Knights carry forth an enduring legacy, shaping not only their lives but also those of the youth they mentor. This chapter explores how these leadership principles empower Knights to rise beyond challenges, fostering environments where teenagers and young adults are encouraged to align their personal potential with their faith journey. In doing so, they create a vibrant community that radiates hope and brings to life the essence of the Theology of the Body.

Developing Leadership Skills

Leadership in the Knights of Columbus isn't just about filling a role or commanding authority; rather, it's about embodying service, fostering community, and nurturing the spiritual growth of oneself and others. The journey of developing leadership skills begins with understanding the core values that guide us as Knights: charity, unity, fraternity, and patriotism. These aren't just catchphrases but are principles that should be deeply ingrained in our actions.

To be an effective leader, one must first understand what it means to lead with authenticity. True leaders inspire respect not by demanding it but by earning it through their integrity and genuine compassion. One way to cultivate these qualities is through consistent self-reflection. This involves regularly examining one's conscience and actions against the teachings of Christ. How often do our daily lives reflect the love and truth of the Gospel? Such introspection is key to growing as a leader who embodies the principles of the Knights of Columbus.

Another fundamental aspect of leadership development in our context is active listening. It's easy to assume that leaders should always be the ones speaking, directing, and instructing. However, true leadership also means being receptive to the voices of others. By creating an environment where dialogue is encouraged and valued, leaders can learn from the diverse experiences and insights of their peers, ultimately fostering a deeper sense of community and mutual respect. This approach not only strengthens personal relationships but also builds a more united and effective council.

Young adults and teenagers, our target audience, are at a crucial stage in life where they are defining who they are and who they will become. Guiding them in leadership development includes empowering them to recognize their unique talents and abilities. Encouraging them to take on small but meaningful roles within their councils can be a powerful way to build confidence. As they grow more comfortable in these roles, their sense of responsibility towards their community and faith is likely to expand.

Mentorship is a crucial element in leadership development among the Knights of Columbus. Established members have the opportunity—and the responsibility—to serve as mentors to younger Knights. Through mentorship, experienced members can share their knowledge, guide new members in understanding the organization's values, and serve as role models in living out their faith. Mentors also play a pivotal role in imparting practical skills such as public speaking, project management, and conflict resolution, which are invaluable in both faith-based activities and professional life.

One cannot discuss leadership without touching on the importance of courage. It takes courage to stand firm in one's faith, particularly in a world that may not always be hospitable to religious convictions. Courage in leadership means being willing to take difficult stands in the face of adversity, showing up for others, and speaking truth even when it's uncomfortable. It is through acts of courage that leaders not only grow in their personal faith but also inspire others to deepen their commitment to their values.

Moreover, today's leaders must navigate the complexities of modern challenges. In a rapidly changing world influenced by technology and media, leaders within the Knights of Columbus must equip themselves with an understanding of these elements to effectively guide the young members. This involves embracing technological tools for communication and organization, leveraging social media for evangelization, and critically evaluating the influences they may have on young minds and hearts.

A vital component of leadership within our ranks is fostering a culture of continuous learning and adaptability. Leaders should encourage themselves and others to participate in workshops, seminars, and retreats offered by the Church or the Knights. These educational opportunities provide essential insights and refresh our understanding of our mission, making us more resilient and effective leaders.

And yet, we must not lose sight of the centrality of prayer. A leader's strength is deeply rooted in their relationship with God. Through prayer and meditation, leaders can maintain their spiritual health, seek wisdom, and receive the grace to confront life's challenges. Emphasizing a prayerful life ensures that leadership is guided by divine insight and compassion, rather than mere human ambition.

Lastly, it's essential to recognize the power of collaboration among Knights. It's tempting to believe that leadership is a solitary endeavor, but the truth is, we are part of a greater narrative. Harnessing the collective strength of diverse talents within the community can lead to achieving goals that might seem daunting when attempted alone. As leaders, we should foster an environment where cooperation is valued and encouraged.

In summary, developing leadership skills within the Knights of Columbus is about nurturing one's personal growth while simultaneously uplifting the community. It's about service, mentorship, courage, and continuous learning, all rooted in a steadfast commitment to faith. By focusing on these aspects, we inch closer to becoming leaders who truly embody the virtues of the Knights of Columbus and, most importantly, of Christ himself.

Leading with Faith and Courage

Leadership calls for a particular kind of strength, one that draws on both faith and courage. At the heart of the Knights of Columbus is an unwavering commitment to these ideals. The men and women of this noble fraternity are often called to lead, not just within their councils but in broader communities, where the values they hold can make a significant difference.

Faith is not a mere accessory to leadership; it's the foundation. Our Catholic faith offers a rich experience of history, tradition, and moral guidance that shapes how leaders act and the paths they choose to follow. But what does it truly mean to lead with faith? It means drawing upon the wisdom of the Church, the courage of saints, and the teachings of Scripture to guide decisions and actions. It's about placing trust in God's plan, even when the road is steep and the destination unclear.

Courage, on the other hand, demands action and resilience. It is about standing firm in convictions, even when the majority stands against them. It is about making difficult choices and sacrifices for the sake of the common good. Leaders within the Knights of Columbus embody this courage, setting examples for others by living out their faith through action.

Imagine a world where leaders are unwavering in their commitment to the virtues of charity, unity, and fraternity, as espoused by our faith. Such leaders don't just inspire; they transform their communities. They serve as shining examples of living out the Gospel in a tangible and impactful way. Drawing on historical figures, contemporary role models, and the teachings of Christ, they change lives.

So, how can young adults and teenagers embrace this call to lead with faith and courage? It begins with education. Understanding the core teachings of the Theology of the Body provides a profound insight into human dignity and purpose. Recognizing that every individual is made in the image of God instills a sense of respect and responsibility in young leaders. This understanding empowers them to foster inclusive and compassionate communities.

It's essential to cultivate courage in a world that often challenges and questions religious beliefs. True courage isn't the absence of fear but the choice to stand firm amidst it. For the Knights of Columbus, this means taking on challenges with a sense of service, mission, and an unshakeable trust in divine providence. This courage is nurtured through communion with others who share the same values, forming bonds that offer strength and support.

Furthermore, leadership is not a solitary journey. Within the Knights, it's about building others up, guiding them with patience and empathy. It's about being attuned to the needs of others and responding with generosity and grace. This community-driven leadership model resonates deeply with the principles of Catholic social teaching, emphasizing the importance of working together towards the common good.

The role of a leader extends beyond decision-making. It is profoundly rooted in being a servant to others. This idea of servant leadership is central to the Knights of Columbus and to Christian leadership as a whole. Serving with humility allows leaders to forge genuine connections and create environments where faith can flourish.

Moreover, developing as a leader involves constant growth and reflection. Even seasoned leaders can learn from the perspectives and experiences of those younger or newer to the faith. Encouraging this exchange is crucial in keeping the organization dynamic and vibrant. Mentorship and shared wisdom are invaluable for nurturing future leaders.

Being a leader today requires engaging with the unique challenges faced by our communities. Whether it's addressing societal issues, promoting justice, or advocating for those without a voice, leadership is an active and dynamic role. The Knights of Columbus are not strangers to such endeavors. As defenders of life, faith, and family, they show that true leadership, grounded in faith and courage, has the power to enact meaningful change.

In conclusion, leading with faith and courage is not just an abstract concept but a lived reality within the Knights of Columbus. By anchoring themselves in their spiritual roots and drawing upon the strength of their community, members can stand as beacons of hope and integrity. They lead by example, inspiring others to follow in their footsteps towards a future built on faith, courage, and love. For any Catholic looking to make a difference, emulating this form of leadership can create a ripple effect, transforming both individuals and the wider society around us.

Conclusion

The journey through the Theology of the Body has been a profound exploration of our faith, a reminder of our calling to live as reflections of God's love in the world. This curriculum aims to provide Roman Catholics, particularly young adults and teenagers, with a deep understanding of their purpose and identity, rooted in their divine creation. The Knights of Columbus play a crucial role as educators and mentors, guiding the youth in embracing these teachings and living out their vocational paths.

In a culture often at odds with faith, the Theology of the Body serves as a beacon of truth and hope. It challenges us to see beyond the superficial, to grasp the sanctity of our bodies, our relationships, and our daily choices. By understanding the intrinsic connection between the body and soul, young people can foster genuine relationships anchored in love and responsibility. This curriculum endeavors to equip them with the tools necessary to discern their vocations, whether that be in marriage, religious life, or single life dedicated to service.

The sacramentality of the body is central to this understanding. Our bodies, temples of the Holy Spirit, call for a life of holiness manifested through personal integrity and virtue. From the embrace of chastity in all life's stages to the recognition of the redemptive nature of suffering, young people are invited to see their lives through the lens of their faith, discovering God's hand at work even in trials.

Furthermore, living in the modern world presents unique challenges that we can't ignore. The pervasive influence of media and technology shapes minds and hearts, often pulling youth away from their spiritual center. Here, the teachings of the Theology of the Body act as a compass. They ground us in truth, helping us navigate these challenges while maintaining a vibrant and authentic faith. The Knights of Columbus' commitment to forming young people into strong, faith-filled leaders is vital, for they are to be the witnesses of hope in their communities.

Knowledge alone isn't sufficient; it must translate into action. Practical applications of these principles make theology accessible and livable. Encouraging engagement with sacraments and diversely expressive art, advocating for life, and leading faith communities are ways in which the curriculum reflects tangible outcomes of learning. By fostering a culture of life and cultivating virtues, young Catholics can live out their faith boldly and effectively.

Moreover, in embracing diversity within the Church, we affirm the global unity embodied by our shared beliefs. This celebration transcends cultural boundaries, enriching the fabric of the Catholic community. Encouraging youth to appreciate this unity can lead to stronger, more inclusive communities, where each person recognizes their inherent value and potential.

As we look to the future, the enduring mission is clear: to unlock the potential of youth through faith, empowering them to set goals aligned with their divine purpose. The Knights of Columbus, in their dedication to leadership and mentorship, are instrumental in this ongoing mission. Through their efforts, young Catholics learn not only to lead but to lead with faith and courage, embodying the principles of the Theology of the Body.

In embracing this curriculum, we affirm our commitment to raising a generation that sees the world through the eyes of faith, with all its beauty, challenges, and opportunities. Together, as a community rooted in Christ's love, we journey forward, inspiring and supporting each other in our shared mission to live out the Gospel in every aspect of our lives.

Appendix A: Prayers for the Journey

Embarking on the journey of understanding and living out the Theology of the Body requires a heart open to prayer and reflection. This appendix provides a collection of prayers tailored for young adults and teenagers, especially those involved with the Knights of Columbus. These prayers aim to nurture spiritual growth, foster personal reflection, and strengthen community bonds as we walk this path of discovery and faith.

1. Prayer for Understanding

Heavenly Father, grant me the wisdom to comprehend Your divine plan for my body and soul. Open my heart to the teachings of Your Holy Church, and help me embrace my unique role in reflecting Your love and truth. Amen.

2. Prayer for Virtue

Lord Jesus, guide me in living a life worthy of my calling. Fill me with courage to pursue virtues of chastity, humility, and kindness. Let my actions be a testament to Your presence in my life. Amen.

3. Prayer for Strength in Community

O Holy Spirit, bind us as a community striving to live out the truths of the Theology of the Body. Strengthen our resolve to support one another, and empower us to be witnesses of Your love and service in the world. Amen.

4. Prayer for Discernment

Mother Mary, gentle guide, help me discern my path in life. As I stand at the crossroads of decision, may your example lead me to embrace my vocation with faith and courage. Intercede for me with your Son, that I may remain faithful to His call. Amen.

5. Prayer for Overcoming Challenges

Saint Joseph, protector and guide, be with me as I navigate the difficulties of modern life. Grant me the perseverance to stay true to my values, even when the world around me tempts me to stray. With your support, may I find comfort and courage in God's eternal promise. Amen.

6. Prayer for Forgiveness and Healing

Savior, grant me the grace to forgive and to seek forgiveness. In moments of hurt and misunderstanding, remind me of Your boundless mercy. Heal the wounds that hinder my journey, and let peace reign in my heart. Amen.

7. Prayer for Daily Commitment

God, You are my source and summit. Help me commit each day to living in accordance with Your will. May my actions reflect Your love, and may I be ever ready to serve those around me with humility and joy. Amen.

These prayers are just a beginning. As you engage with the Theology of the Body, may these words inspire you to deepen your own prayer life and seek a closer relationship with God. Use these prayers as a foundation, but also be open to how the Holy Spirit may guide you to new forms of prayer and meditation. Let the journey of faith be one of continuous growth, connection, and discovery.

Appendix B: Additional Resources for Further Study

Embarking on a journey to understand the Theology of the Body is a profound and enlightening experience. To deepen this understanding, it's valuable to explore additional resources that offer varied perspectives and insights. Here, we've compiled a list of resources that will support further study and reflection for Roman Catholics, Knights of Columbus, young adults, and teenagers.

Books and Publications

- "Theology of the Body Explained" by Christopher West: This book offers a comprehensive exploration of Pope Saint John Paul II's teachings and makes complex theological concepts accessible.

- "Man and Woman He Created Them: A Theology of the Body" by Pope Saint John Paul II: The original texts of the Theology of the Body offer deep insights into human dignity and divine love.
- "Love and Responsibility" by Karol Wojtyla (Pope Saint John Paul II): An essential precursor to the Theology of the Body, this book discusses the ethical teachings on human love.

Online Courses and Lectures

- The Theology of the Body Institute: Offers courses and retreats that delve into the teachings, enabling participants to experience personal transformation and growth.
- Ascension Presents: A platform for engaging video content, including lectures on the Theology of the Body and its application in modern life.

Documentaries and Video Resources

- "Humanum Series": This documentary series explores various aspects of human identity and relationships, aligning closely with the principles of the Theology of the Body.
- Christopher West's YouTube Channel: Features a range of talks and short videos that explore the dynamic ways Theology of the Body interacts with everyday life.

Websites and Online Communities

- Theology of the Body for Teens (TOB Teens): An initiative to engage teenagers with concepts that are both relatable and transformative.
- Chastity Project: Directed by Jason and Crystalina Evert, it provides excellent resources and community support for living out the virtue of chastity.

Workshops and Seminars

- The National Theology of the Body Congress: An opportunity to join enthusiasts and scholars in exploring the profound teachings of the Theology of the Body through talks and interactive sessions.
- Knights of Columbus Parish Seminars: Local councils often organize seminars that can serve as both an introduction and an advanced study into these teachings.

These resources offer a foundation for expanding one's knowledge and practical application of the Theology of the Body. As you engage with these materials, remember that this study is not just an academic exercise; it's a call to live out these truths daily, with courage and compassion, within your community and beyond.

Appendix C: Contact Information for Support and Guidance

Embarking on the journey of understanding and integrating the Theology of the Body into one's life can be both rewarding and challenging. We recognize the essential role that support and guidance play in this path. For this reason, we've compiled contact resources to ensure you are never alone in your journey. These resources are here to assist Knights of Columbus members, young adults, and teenagers in deepening their faith and understanding.

1. Knights of Columbus Resources

- Local Councils: Visit the Find a Council section on the Knights of Columbus website to connect with a local council. There's a thriving community ready to support you.
- Faith Formation Committees: Reach out to your council's Faith Formation Committee to engage in discussions, events, and study groups centered around the Theology of the Body.

2. Church and Parish Contacts

- Parish Priests and Clergy: Your parish priest is a valuable resource. They're often eager to support your spiritual journey and can provide personal guidance or direct you to appropriate resources.
- Diocesan Offices: Most dioceses have offices dedicated to youth ministry and catechesis that can offer materials and guidance. Contact them for local support networks.

3. Online Resources and Helplines

- Theology of the Body Institute: This organization offers courses, retreats, and resources. Visit their website to access online content or join a workshop.
- Support Helplines: Many dioceses and faith-based organizations offer helplines for immediate pastoral care and advice.

We've been given a tremendous gift in the Theology of the Body, one that invites us to see with new eyes the profound dignity and purpose for which we are created. Remember, whether you're facing questions or simply seeking to grow deeper in faith, the community and resources are here to guide and support you every step of the way. Don't hesitate to reach out and connect with those who can walk this beautiful journey with you.